The
Source®
for
Asperger's Syndrome

Timothy P. Kowalski

Content Area:	Asperger's Syndrome
Ages:	All Ages

LinguiSystems, Inc.
3100 4th Avenue
East Moline, IL 61244-9700
1-800-PRO IDEA
1-800-776-4332

FAX: 1-800-577-4555
E-mail: service@linguisystems.com
Web: www.linguisystems.com
TDD: 1-800-933-8331
(for those with hearing impairments)

Printed in the U.S.A.

ISBN 0-7606-0473-8

About the Author

Timothy P. Kowalski, M.A., CCC/SLP, has a speech-language pathology practice in Winter Park, Florida. He has extensive experience in treating individuals within the autistic spectrum and has spoken extensively on this topic nationally and internationally. In addition to treating individuals in his office, he also provides consultation to academic facilities for children with developmental and autistic spectrum disabilities in both inclusive and self-contained settings. He was named "TEAMS 2000 Speech-Language Pathologist of the Year" for his work with autism in the four-county greater Orlando region.

Tim resides in Orlando, Florida, with his wife, who also is a speech-language pathologist and a partner in their practice. They have two children, Laura and Matthew.

The Source for Asperger's Syndrome is Tim's first publication with LinguiSystems.

➢ Dedication

To my family and friends, for their encouragement and suggestions throughout this endeavor, and most importantly, to those individuals with Asperger's Syndrome

Cover Design by Mike Paustian
Page Layout by Lisa Parker
Edited by Carolyn LoGiudice

Table of Contents

Introduction 7

Chapter 1: Diagnostic Criteria
The Faces of Asperger's 9
Major Classifications of Characteristics. 11
DSM-IV TR 12
ICD-10 14
Gillberg's Criteria 16

Chapter 2: Epidemiology
Prevalence. 24
Comorbidity 24
Causal Factors. 25

Chapter 3: Diagnosis & Misdiagnosis
Diagnosis 26
Historical Information 26
Psychological Examination 27
Communication Assessment 28
Rating Scales and Profiles 32
Misdiagnosis. 35
Differential Diagnosis 36
Description of Specific Disorders 39

Chapter 4: Case History 44

Chapter 5: Theory of Mind 57

Chapter 6: Social & Emotional Issues
Skills & Deficits 61
Social Interaction 61
Social Rules 62
Gullibility 63
Egocentricity. 63
Literal Interpretation of Messages 65
Prosodic Information. 65
Lack of Tact 66

Table of Contents, *continued*

Proxemics 67
Conversation 68
Inappropriate Behavior 69
Sensory Integration 69
Consistency and Conformity 70
Facing the Unknown 73
Rigidity: An Ineffective Coping Strategy 74
Social/Emotional Checklist 77
Treatment Strategies 80
Direct Instruction for Social Skills 80
Alternative Instruction 80
Nonverbal Language 81
Changing Social Behavior 82
Individualized, Immediate Feedback 82
Abstract Language 83
Individualized Instruction 83
Structured Play Groups 83
Taking Others' Perspectives 84
Focusing Attention 85
Small-Group Activities 85
Cooperation and Compromise 86
Capitalizing on Strengths 88
Conversation Training 88
Eye Contact 90
Self-Confidence 91
Predictability 92
Classroom Group Interaction 92
Environmental Organization 93
"Safety" 93
Transitions 94
Scheduling Tools 94
Checklists 97
Daily Routines 97
Surprises and the Unknown 97
Expanding Interest Range 98

Table of Contents, *continued*

Suggestions for Intervention 102
   Social-Interactive. 102
   Social-Communicative. 103
   Social-Emotional 104

Chapter 7: Academic Issues
Skills & Deficits 106
   Attending 106
   Reading. 107
   Classroom Discussions 107
   Time Management and Organization 108
   Motor Difficulties 109
   Comprehension 111
   Abstract Thinking 111
   Inadequate Diagnoses 112
   Social Interaction. 113
Academic Checklist. 115
Treatment Strategies 118
   Engaging in Tasks 119
   Consistent Success 120
   Task Completion 120
   Reading Comprehension 123
   Motor Deficits. 125
   Adapting the Curriculum. 126
   Modifying the Environment. 127
   Thinking Skills 129
   Unwritten Rules at School. 134
Teaching Techniques. 135

Chapter 8: Prognosis 140

References 142

Introduction

Asperger's Syndrome is not just a high-functioning variant of autism. It presents with a variety of symptoms unique unto itself. Too often, we recognize the parts but not the whole. As a result, Asperger's Syndrome is frequently misdiagnosed by well-intentioned diagnosticians, causing untold problems for the child, his family, and his school. Asperger's Syndrome brings numerous challenges to everyone involved, including professionals.

I once had a professor who refused to accept any papers on autism because he did not believe anything could be done for these individuals. Thankfully, history has proven him wrong. Individuals presenting with autistic spectrum disorders can, and do, benefit from intervention — if proper treatment is provided.

A parent once wrote to the editor of an autism journal seeking input as to the best placement for her child. Should it be a self-contained classroom for autism or an inclusion classroom? The editor stated that individual factors specific to the child would best determine placement. However, he also stated that having knowledgeable educators for the child was the most important factor influencing the outcome in autism intervention.

When I first started working with high-functioning children within the autism spectrum, these children were basically defined as either *classic Kanner-style autistic* or *high-functioning autistic*. As my caseload grew, I began to notice a significant difference among the high-functioning population. Their so-called *patterns of consistency* were not consistent. Over time, I learned about the differences between autism and Asperger's Syndrome and immersed myself in the literature to better understand the unique characteristics found in this population.

In the course of my research, I found few sources available to assist the practitioner in the diagnosis and treatment of Asperger's Syndrome. The need for a non-technical resource soon became apparent. *The Source for Asperger's Syndrome* is designed specifically to fill that need. This book is a comprehensive source of information written in a language designed to allow the reader to quickly grasp its content. Starting with snapshots of children, Chapters 1 and 2 present an overview of the problem now known as *Asperger's Syndrome*. Chapters 3 and 4 enable diagnosticians to see the

proverbial "forest through the trees" and, hopefully, avoid an all-too-frequent misdiagnosis.

All practitioners working with this population need to have an understanding of Uta Frith's "Theory of Mind." Chapter 5 presents this concept in a down-to-earth manner, thereby allowing the reader to recognize how this theory relates to everything the child with Asperger's Syndrome does. Chapters 6 and 7 present practical, skill-based information all practitioners yearn for. Chapter 8 addresses every parent's concern about what the future holds for his/her child.

The Source for Asperger's Syndrome is designed for those who have contact with these unique individuals. Parents, educators, diagnosticians, physicians, and administrators will find the information useful in addressing the needs of these children. I hope you find it practical, easy, and, most importantly, useful.

Tim Kowalski

Chapter 1:
Diagnostic Criteria

➤ The Faces of Asperger's

Thomas walks into the office, Game Boy™ in hand. He is a striking adolescent with light-brown hair and dark-brown eyes. He appears to be a typical eleven-year-old — that is, until you begin to converse with him. Then you realize this eleven-year-old boy is far from typical.

Thomas introduces himself and quickly begins a discussion on telephone poles; their height, composition, fabrication, and life expectancy. He provides you with the greatest detail about these common objects and is oblivious to the fact that you are completely uninterested. Your nonverbal cues designed to indicate a desire to discontinue the topic have no effect on him, in part because he frequently is looking everywhere except at you, and when he does glance your way, he remains unaware of your displeasure. Despite your noticeable discomfort, he continues with his lecture. By now, the stares of onlookers have given way to outright laughter as it becomes more obvious that Thomas is not about to stop.

To the unknowing, Thomas is perceived as rude, bad-mannered, and inconsiderate; traits not known for making and keeping friends. Despite his keen desire to establish conversation, Thomas fails to achieve the intended result and continues his one-sided conversation, only serving to provide his onlookers with more topics of discussion about his inappropriate behavior.

Susan is a bright, happy, eight-year-old girl whose demeanor changes drastically when she is stressed. She has few friends and those she considers "friends" appear to be several years younger than she. Simple tasks, such as writing spelling words and multiplication tables, have the capacity to provoke award-winning temper tantrums. Once such an outburst begins, the chances of rapidly stopping it are minimal, at best. Susan has been referred to the child study team with hopes that the behavior specialist can develop an appropriate behavior plan for her.

Jimmy enters the office with a large smile. He just saw the movie *Toy Story* and is now totally absorbed in anything related to that movie. In his hand is his current favorite toy, Woody, one of the movie's main characters. Jimmy flits around the room, holding Woody, but instead of engaging this character in pretend conversations or situations, Jimmy is intent on playing only with Woody's cowboy hat. When asked what he is doing, Jimmy replies in grammatically correct speech that he's playing with his toy. The manner in which he speaks, however, is noticeably peculiar in both rhythm and pitch. This odd speaking manner does not seem to be dysfluency but an inappropriate use of suprasegmental speech features. Jimmy quickly returns to Woody's hat and fails to notice the other children in the room until someone comes in with another *Toy Story* character. Then Jimmy's eyes open wide. He runs over to the child and begins to deliver a complete scene-by-scene retelling of the entire movie.

Robert, a veritable fount of wisdom with respect to Pokemon™, delights in sharing his Pokemon™ cards with his ten-year-old classmates. Unfortunately, he demands that each of his friends perform according to his scripted routines and becomes highly agitated when they do not play according to the rules he makes and the roles he ascribes. When his friends attempt to change the topic or engage Robert in some other activity, he resists. Repeated attempts by his friends fail to change Robert's idea of how to play. The result is typically an explosive episode. Later that day he wonders why his friends didn't play with him. After all, they were having fun.

These are the faces of *Asperger's Syndrome*, a term given to those children first described by the Austrian physician Hans Asperger in 1944 (Asperger, 1944). In his published paper, written in German towards the end of World War II, Asperger specifically described four children who were said to represent a much larger population. He described them as having social ineptitude, an insistence on sameness, nonverbal language deficiencies, alterations in affect, and stereotyped behaviors. Interestingly, he published his paper one year after Leo Kanner's landmark article on autism (Kanner, 1943). Remarkably, neither man was aware of the other's work.

Insightful as Asperger's article was, the turmoil of World War II did not allow him to receive worldwide recognition until Lorna Wing

translated it into English. Only then did professionals begin to recognize the similarities with which these children presented. Researchers were beginning to notice that the fundamental difference between the Asperger-style children and the Kanner-style children was the presence in Asperger-style children of grammatically correct language in early childhood. It was further recognized that this language did not appear intended for interpersonal social interaction (Wing, 1981; Wing, 1991; Cumine et al., 1998).

➤ Major Classifications of Characteristics

To this day, scholars continue to debate whether Asperger's Syndrome is indeed a distinct classification or a subcategory of autism. Differential diagnosis has improved somewhat now that Asperger's Syndrome is represented in two major classification systems of diseases and disabilities.

According to the *Diagnostic and Statistical Manual of Mental Disorders, Fourth Edition, Text Revised (DSM-IV TR)*, *Asperger's Syndrome* is a term for one of five specific disorders classified as *Pervasive Developmental Disorder (PDD)* (American Psychiatric Association, 1994). For a child to be labeled with a diagnosis of *Asperger's Syndrome*, he must present with a variety of deficits that, when viewed as a whole, differentiate him from other PDDs. This is consistent with the *Tenth Revision of the International Classification of Disease (ICD-10)*, published by the World Health Organization (World Health Organization, 1989). Each of these institutions has published a set of criteria now widely used to assist in differential diagnosis of Asperger's (pages 12-15).

Yet another set of criteria was developed by Christopher Gillberg (Gillberg and Gillberg, 1989), listed on pages 16 and 17. Gillberg noticed similarities among children who did not fit the classic Kanner description of autism. He published his findings in 1989. Gillberg recognized that these children presented with extreme egocentricity and were generally uninterested in another individual's views or interests. Not only did these children have an inability to interact with their peers, they also often failed to respond to the cues provided by others and frequently exhibited inappropriate social and emotional responses. Gillberg also noted they often had extremely limited interests and were preoccupied with trivial details that appeared to be more rote memorization than meaningful information. These children imposed repetitive routines or rituals on both themselves and others and had peculiar speech and language.

Many of these children evidenced a delay in developing language skills as infants. Superficially they appeared to possess perfect expressive language, but their speech prosody was odd. Their abstract language skills evidenced confusion in the areas of literal and implied meanings. Nonverbal communication problems were evident in their limited use of gestures and their clumsy body language. The facial expressions of these children were frequently inappropriate, often demonstrating a peculiar, stiff gaze. These children also evidenced difficulty with physical proximity. Motor clumsiness, Gillberg determined, was not always apparent in these children.

All three of the previously described classification systems are listed below and on the following pages. Note that Gillberg's criteria echo those published by the American Psychiatric Association and the World Health Organization, but they offer more insight into the communication deficits these children present.

DSM-IV TR

A. Qualitative impairment in social interaction, as manifested by at least two of the following:

1. Marked impairment in the use of multiple nonverbal behaviors such as eye-to-eye gaze, facial expression, body postures, and gestures to regulate social interaction

2. Failure to develop peer relationships appropriate to developmental level

3. A lack of spontaneous seeking to share enjoyment, interests, or achievements with other people

4. Lack of social or emotional reciprocity

B. Restricted repetitive and stereotyped patterns of behavior, interests, and activities, as manifested by at least one of the following:

   1. Encompassing preoccupation with one or more stereotyped and restricted patterns of interest that is abnormal either in intensity or focus

   2. Apparently inflexible adherence to specific, nonfunctional routines or rituals

   3. Stereotyped and repetitive motor mannerisms

   4. Persistent preoccupation with parts or objects

C. The disturbance causes clinically significant impairment in social, occupational, or other important areas of functioning.

D. There is no clinically significant general delay in language.

E. There is no clinically significant delay in cognitive development or in the development of age-appropriate self-help skills, adaptive behavior (other than social interactions), and curiosity about the environment in childhood.

F. Criteria are not met for another specific Pervasive Developmental Disorder or Schizophrenia.

Reprinted with permission from the *Diagnostic and Statistical Manual of Mental Disorders, Fourth Edition, Text Revision.* Copyright 2000 American Psychiatric Association.

Chapter 1: Diagnostic Criteria
The Source for Asperger's Syndrome
            13

ICD-10

A. There is no clinically significant general delay in spoken or receptive language or cognitive development. Diagnosis requires that single words should have developed by 2 years of age or earlier and that communicative phrases be used by 3 years of age or earlier. Self-help skills, adaptive behavior, and curiosity about the environment during the first 3 years should be at a level consistent with normal intellectual development. However, motor milestones may be somewhat delayed and motor clumsiness is usual (although not a necessary diagnostic feature). Isolated special skills, often related to abnormal preoccupations, are common, but are not required for diagnosis.

B. Qualitative abnormalities in reciprocal social interaction are manifest in at least two of the following areas:

1. Failure to adequately use eye-to-eye gaze, facial expression, body posture, and gesture to regulate social interaction;

2. Failure to develop (in a manner appropriate to mental age, and despite ample opportunities) peer relationships that involve a mutual sharing of interests, activities and emotions;

3. Lack of socio-emotional reciprocity as shown by an impairment or deviant response to other people's emotions; or lack of modulation of behavior according to social context; or a weak integration of social, emotional, and communicative behaviors;

4. Lack of spontaneous seeking to share enjoyment, interests, or achievements with other people (e.g., a lack of showing, bringing, or pointing out to other people objects of interest to the individual).

C. The individual exhibits an unusually intense, circumscribed interest or restricted, repetitive and stereotyped patterns of behavior, interests, and activities manifested in at least one of the following areas:

1. An encompassing preoccupation with stereotyped and restricted patterns of interest that are abnormal in content or focus; or one or more interests that are abnormal in their intensity and circumscribed nature though not in the content or focus;

2. Apparently compulsive adherence to specific, non-functional routines or rituals;

3. Stereotyped and repetitive motor mannerisms that involve either hand/finger flapping or twisting or complex whole-body movements;

4. Preoccupations with part-objects or non-functional elements of play materials (such as their color, the feel of their surface, or the noise/vibration that they generate); however, it would be less usual for these to include either motor mannerisms or preoccupations with part-objects or non-functional elements of play materials.

D. The disorder is not attributable to the other varieties of pervasive developmental disorder: simple schizophrenia, schizo-typal disorder, obsessive-compulsive disorder, anankastic personality disorder, reactive and disinhibited attachment disorders of childhood.

Reprinted with permission from the *Tenth Revision of the International Classification of Disease*, Geneva, World Health Organization, 1989.

Gillberg's Criteria

A. Social impairment with extreme egocentricity

　1. Inability to interact with peers

　2. Poor appreciation of social cues

　3. Inappropriate social and emotional responses

B. Limited interests and preoccupation

　1. More rote than meaning

　2. Exclusive of other interests

　3. Repetitive adherence

C. Repetitive routines or rituals

　1. Imposed on self

　2. Imposed on others

D. Speech and language peculiarities

　1. Delayed early development possible

　2. Superficially perfect expressive language

　3. Odd prosody, peculiar voice

　4. Impaired comprehension, especially with literal and implied meanings

E. Nonverbal communication problems

    1. Limited use of gestures

    2. Clumsy body language

    3. Inappropriate facial expression

    4. Difficulty with physical proximity

F. Motor clumsiness may not always be seen.

How, then, does the practitioner determine which set of criteria to use when attempting to diagnosis a child suspected of possessing Asperger's Syndrome? Table 1, pages 18-21, is a quick representation of the three major classification systems available to date. It provides an opportunity to compare the criteria published in the *DSM-IV TR*, *ICD-10*, and Gillberg's Criteria.

Table 1:
Comparison of Three Major Classification Systems for Asperger's Syndrome

DSM-IV TR	*ICD-10*	**Gillberg's Criteria**
Qualitative impairment in social interaction (A)*	Qualitative abnormalities in reciprocal social interaction (B)*	Social impairment with extreme egocentricity (A)*
Marked impairment in the use of multiple nonverbal behaviors such as eye-to-eye gaze, facial expression, body postures, and gestures to regulate social interaction (A1)*	Failure to adequately use eye-to-eye gaze, facial expression, body posture, and gesture to regulate social interaction (B1)*	Poor appreciation of social cues (A2)*
Failure to develop peer relationships appropriate to developmental level (A2)*	Failure to develop (in a manner appropriate to mental age, despite ample opportunities) peer relationships that involve mutual sharing of interests, activities and emotions (B2)*	Inability to interact with peers (A1)*
A lack of spontaneous seeking to share enjoyment, interests, or achievements with other people (A3)*	Lack of spontaneous seeking to share enjoyment, interests, or achievements with other people (e.g., a lack of showing, bringing, or pointing out to other people objects of interest to the individual) (B4)*	
Lack of social or emotional reciprocity (A4)*	Lack of socio-emotional reciprocity as shown by an impairment or deviant response to other people's emotions; or lack of modulation of behavior according to social context; or a weak integration of social, emotional, and communicative behaviors (B3)*	Inappropriate social and emotional responses (A3)*

* Letters and numbers in parentheses in this table refer to the corresponding outline designations on pages 12-17. The *DSM-IV TR* column follows the original order of this information.

DSM-IV TR	ICD-10	Gillberg's Criteria
Restricted repetitive and stereotyped patterns of behavior, interests, and activities (B)*	The individual exhibits an unusually intense, circumscribed interest or restricted, repetitive and stereotyped patterns of behavior, interests, and activities. (C)*	Limited interests and preoccupation (B)* More rote than meaning (B1)* Repetitive adherence (B3)*
Encompassing preoccupation with one or more stereotyped and restricted patterns of interest that is abnormal either in intensity or focus (B1)*	An encompassing preoccupation with stereotyped and restricted patterns of interest that are abnormal in content or focus; or one or more interests that are abnormal in their intensity and circumscribed nature though not in the content or focus (C1)*	More rote than meaning (B1)* Exclusive of other interests (B2)*
Apparently inflexible adherence to specific, nonfunctional routines or rituals (B2)*	Apparently compulsive adherence to specific, nonfunctional routines or rituals (C2)*	Repetitive routines or rituals (C)* Imposed on self (C1)* Imposed on others (C2)*
Stereotyped and repetitive motor mannerisms (B3)*	Stereotyped and repetitive motor mannerisms that involve hand/finger flapping or twisting or complex whole-body movements (C3)*	
Persistent preoccupation with parts or objects (B4)*	Preoccupation with part-objects or non-functional elements of play materials (such as their color, the feel of their surface, or the noise/vibration that they generate) (C4)*	

* Letters and numbers in parentheses in this table refer to the corresponding outline designations on pages 12-17. The *DSM-IV TR* column follows the original order of this information.

DSM-IV TR	ICD-10	Gillberg's Criteria
The disturbance causes clinically significant impairment in social, occupational, or other important areas of functioning. (C)*		Inappropriate social and emotional responses (A)*
There is no clinically significant delay in language. (D)*	There is no clinically significant general delay in spoken or receptive language. Diagnosis requires that single words should have developed by 2 years of age or earlier and that communicative phrases be used by 3 years of age or earlier. (A)*	Delayed early language is possible. (D1)* Impaired comprehension, especially with literal and implied meanings (D4)*
There is no clinically significant delay in cognitive development or in the development of age-appropriate self-help skills, adaptive behavior (other than in social interaction), and curiosity about the environment in childhood. (E)*	There is no clinically significant general delay in cognitive development. Self-help skills, adaptive behavior, and curiosity about the environment during the first 3 years should be at a level consistent with normal intellectual development. (A)*	
Criteria not met for another specific Pervasive Development Disorder or Schizophrenia (F)*	The disorder is not attributable to the other varieties of pervasive developmental disorder: simple schizophrenia, schizotypal disorder, obsessive-compulsive disorder, anankastic personality disorder, reactive and disinhibited attachment disorders of childhood. (D)*	

* Letters and numbers in parentheses in this table refer to the corresponding outline designations on pages 12-17. The *DSM-IV TR* column follows the original order of this information.

DSM-IV TR	ICD-10	Gillberg's Criteria
	Motor milestones may be somewhat delayed and motor clumsiness is usual, although not a necessary diagnostic feature. (A)*	Motor clumsiness may not always be seen. (F)*
		Speech and language peculiarities (D)* Superficially perfect expressive language (D2)* Odd prosody, peculiar voice (D3)*
		Nonverbal communication problems (E)* Limited use of gestures (E1)* Clumsy body language (E2)* Inappropriate facial expression (E3)* Difficulty with physical proximity (E4)*
Reprinted with permission from the *Diagnostic and Statistical Manual of Mental Disorders, Fourth Edition, Text Revision.* Copyright 2000 American Psychiatric Association.	Reprinted with permission from the *Tenth Revision of the International Classification of Disease*, Geneva, World Health Organization, 1989.	Gillberg and Gillberg, 1989

* Letters and numbers in parentheses in this table refer to the corresponding outline designations on pages 12-17. The *DSM-IV TR* column follows the original order of this information.

Note that all three systems report deficits in social interaction with specific reference to recognizing social cues, including eye-to-eye gaze, facial expressions, postures, and gestures. All three classification systems also define social interaction deficits as difficulties in developing appropriate peer interactions and relationships. While Gillberg does not reference an inability to spontaneously seek to share enjoyment and interests with others, this trait is mentioned in both the *DSM-IV TR* and *ICD-10*. Social and emotional issues are also cited by all three classification systems. Each one indicates inappropriate use or a lack of social and emotional reciprocity.

In addition to deficits in social interaction, all three systems indicate the presence of a narrow interest range that limits the individual's ability to interact with others. This restricted interest range is manifested by an unusually intense interest in specific topics the child may impose upon himself or others.

The *DSM-IV TR* and *ICD-10* both include references to unusual motor mannerisms and preoccupations with parts of objects. This symptom is not specified in Gillberg's criteria.

Discrepancy exists between Gillberg's criteria and both the *DSM-IV TR* and *ICD-10* regarding the presence of language delay. According to Gillberg's criteria, early language may be delayed, whereas both the *DSM-IV TR* and *ICD-10* indicate that no clinically significant delay is present in language development. However, research is beginning to consider Asperger's Syndrome as a possible diagnosis, even with the presence of a language delay (Bonus et al., 1997; Eisenmajer et al., 1998; Mayes and Calhoun, 2001).

As with language delay, controversy exists concerning cognitive skills (Bonus et al., 1997; Eisenmajer et al., 1998). Both the *DSM-IV TR* and *ICD-10* indicate that no delays in cognitive development are present. Gillberg's criteria do not specifically refer to cognitive development, but they do indicate that comprehension of implied meanings is impaired. Although this impairment is not a true cognitive deficiency, the deficits noted in spontaneous conversation may give the impression of cognitive deficiency.

The criteria for Asperger's Syndrome found in both the *DSM-IV TR* and the *ICD-10* are but one part of a comprehensive manual used for diagnosing a wide variety of disorders. Both publications indicate that Asperger's Syndrome cannot be considered if the individual's symptoms can be better attributed to another disorder.

Chapter 1: Diagnostic Criteria
The Source for Asperger's Syndrome   22

Motor deficits, specifically clumsiness, are reported in both the *ICD-10* and Gillberg's criteria but are not mentioned in the *DSM-IV TR*.

Only Gillberg's criteria delineates the speech and language deficits seen in Asperger's Syndrome. He specifies that a person with Asperger's Syndrome presents with superficially perfect expressive language but may exhibit an odd prosody and/or peculiar voice. Gillberg also addresses the nonverbal communication deficits frequently seen in this population. His criteria note limited use of gestures and clumsy body language often seen in these individuals as well as difficulties with facial expression and physical proximity.

By closely analyzing an individual's symptoms, an astute diagnostician may accurately identify those traits attributed to Asperger's Syndrome.

Chapter 2:
Epidemiology

➢ Prevalence

Actual prevalence figures for Asperger's Syndrome are difficult to determine. Perhaps the best figures provided come from the Swedish study performed by Ehlers and Gillberg in 1993 (Ehlers and Gillberg, 1993). They studied children in mainstream education and concluded that children diagnosed with Asperger's Syndrome presented with a prevalence rate of 36 per 10,000 children. They further speculated that this figure is most likely low due to the large numbers of children misdiagnosed or underserved. In 1999 a study was undertaken of seven-year-old children to determine if the rate of Asperger's Syndrome had changed from previous studies (Kadesjo et al., 1999). Findings did not differ widely from earlier studies with rates of 48 per 10,000 children.

Another study cited approximately 20-25 children per every 10,000 presented with Asperger's Syndrome whereas four-to-five children per every 10,000 presented with classic autism (Fombonne, 1996).

All prevalence studies maintain Asperger's Syndrome is much more common in boys than in girls. Gillberg postulated that the ratio of boys to girls is approximately ten-to-one whereas Asperger believed it to be exclusive to boys (Gillberg, 1991).

➢ Comorbidity

As with autism, comorbidity is frequently common with Asperger's Syndrome (Gillberg and Billstedt, 2000; Kadesjo and Gillberg, 2000). Tourette's disorder, ADHD, and mood disorders, specifically depression and anxiety, are all frequently seen in children diagnosed with Asperger's Syndrome.

 # Causal Factors

While causal factors remain uncertain, it is generally accepted that Asperger's Syndrome is a neurological disorder. Research continues to advance this hypothesis and, as technology improves, may someday determine the actual cause of Asperger's Syndrome.

There is frequently a genetic component to Asperger's Syndrome. Asperger himself described it as an "inherited personality disorder" when theorizing a genetic link. Although Asperger's Syndrome is not viewed as directly inherited, current research has identified a genetic basis to the syndrome. In many children studied, the father often presents with a full picture of Asperger's Syndrome. Relatives frequently evidence temperamental traits characterized by intense and limited interest, compulsive or rigid styles of interaction, social awkwardness, and timidity. Some may be diagnosed with classic autism. Many relatives evidence a high rate of depression, both bipolar and unipolar.

Chapter 3:
Diagnosis & Misdiagnosis

➤ Diagnosis

The diagnosis of Asperger's Syndrome presents with significant difficulties that are directly related to the subjective measures being applied. As more diagnosticians become familiar with autistic spectrum disorders, they will invariably be presented with children who do not fit the standard *autistic* label. Only through careful investigation will the children presenting with Asperger's Syndrome receive the appropriate label.

It is crucial to obtain a differential diagnosis when attempting to evaluate children presumed to present with Asperger's Syndrome. All assessments should include the following information.

Historical Information

A comprehensive investigation into the child's early developmental progress allows for greater accuracy in diagnosis. Such an investigation should include, but not be limited to, the age and nature of the onset, along with medical and family history. Details regarding developmental milestones, the presence of any regression in early childhood, and associated information relative to diagnostic determiners should be ascertained. Family history, both nuclear and extended, should be reviewed with respect to the presence of mental retardation, Fragile X Syndrome, and tuberous sclerosis. In addition, the presence of psychiatric concerns should also be investigated.

Psychological Examination

A comprehensive psychological evaluation is warranted to obtain estimates of intellectual functioning. To obtain such information, the diagnostician measures the child's ability to perform factual information, such as vocabulary and mathematics; higher-level abstract thinking and reasoning, such as verbal and nonverbal reasoning and problem solving; as well as memory and speed of recall. The majority of instruments available today measure these skills in a variety of means and differ from one another by the influence linguistic skills have on test construction.

Since children with Asperger's Syndrome have excellent rote memory skills and difficulties in abstract reasoning and literal interpretation, the diagnostician should use caution when interpreting results so as not to present bias based on isolated strengths and weaknesses. In many instances where extremely inconsistent and contradictory scores have been averaged, a false representation of the intellectual profile has resulted.

In general, cognitive profiles for Asperger's Syndrome differ from lower-functioning autism in that the verbal scores are often higher than performance scores (Ehlers et al., 1997). Asperger's Syndrome is further differentiated from autism by significantly higher verbal mental age. There is a concern, however, that the *DSM-IV TR* and *ICD-10* criteria for Asperger's Syndrome are not sensitive enough to fully describe the communication domain (Eisenmajer et al., 1996). Tasks involving empathy have been found useful to discriminate both Asperger's Syndrome and autism from individuals with no psychological disorder (Dyck et al., 2001), with both groups performing significantly poorer on any empathic measure.

Peaks are often seen in verbally mediated tasks while tasks requiring visual-perceptual speed involving motor output are often weak (Klin et al., 2000). Standardized testing using the *WISC-R* (Wechsler, 1979) of individuals with Asperger's Syndrome has shown strengths on verbal ability subtests and deficits on Object Assembly and Coding Subtests (Ehlers et al., 1997). Many individuals with Asperger's Syndrome also evidence higher performance on tasks involving nonverbal problem solving (Klin et al., 2000).

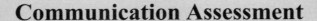

Communication Assessment

A complete analysis of receptive and expressive language skills, including nonverbal communication and pragmatic use of language, is of utmost importance in assessing children who potentially have Asperger's Syndrome. Social and communicative competence should also be assessed as they relate to nonverbal intellectual abilities. All assessment techniques should take into consideration the varying abilities present according to the manner in which the data is obtained. Evaluation should include standardized instruments, naturalistic observations, parental interviews, and procedures designed specifically to assess social-pragmatic functioning.

Speech-language pathologists have typically been challenged to find standardized tools that specifically assess deficient communication in nonverbal communication and pragmatic use of language. School-based clinicians are further restricted by district-based requirements that often bar providing services that would benefit many children with Asperger's Syndrome. Unfortunately, many districts require an instrument that provides a global communication score. Since children with Asperger's Syndrome usually have strengths in syntax and semantics, they often score adequately on such global instruments. These tests do not include accurate measures of social appropriateness, so the real deficits in this area go undetected or unverified via formal assessment. Students with Asperger's Syndrome who need speech-language services may not qualify under strict testing requirements. The astute diagnostician should, instead, attempt to gather data from a variety of instruments that will support or refute the hypothesis of Asperger's Syndrome.

Using subtests that probe for higher-language thought processing may provide important information for the diagnostician. Superficial language use often appears adequate in children with Asperger's Syndrome, yet many of them rely on rote learning and fail to fully grasp the complete picture of everyday situations, classroom lessons, or reading passages. This over-reliance on rote learning becomes more noticeable in upper grades, where reading for content is of critical concern. In addition, idiomatic expressions that are readily understood by most students, may confuse students with Asperger's Syndrome. Humor, with its reliance on double meanings and sarcasm, is also a source of frustration for these youngsters.

While not standardized, pragmatic analyses of language provide the most meaningful source of diagnostic information. Several of these tools are described below and on the following pages. These instruments make it possible to analyze a wide variety of social language use. While none of these assessments offers the complete answer to the diagnostician, each instrument provides unique insight into the communication problems associated with Asperger's Syndrome.

Dore's Conversational Acts

Designed as a method to analyze the communicative function an utterance possesses, *Dore's Conversational Acts* allows the diagnostician to assess an utterance based on not only the form of the utterance, but also its use in discourse. Dore describes a conversational act as possessing these three components (Stickler, 1987):

> ➤ Propositional Content — the utterance's meaning; the basic information within the content of the utterance

> ➤ Grammatical Structure — the syntactic nature of the utterance

> ➤ Illocutionary Function — the intent of the speaker

For a speaker to communicate effectively, each speech act must include these three elements and use them appropriately.

The diagnostician may use *Dore's Conversational Acts* to differentiate a speaker's utterances into seven subcategories. A miscellaneous category is also included for utterances that are unintelligible, incomplete, or lacking propositional intent. While not standardized, Dore's analysis affords the quantification of conversational acts based on their pragmatic use. By analyzing the types of conversational acts employed, a diagnostician can develop a picture that details the relative strengths and weaknesses present in the speaker's utterances. Patterns of use may be discerned and compared to the speaker's same-aged peers to establish a measure of pragmatic proficiency.

Halliday's Functions of Language

Using seven categories, Halliday's *Functions of Language* categorizes a child's emerging use of language according to longitudinal developmental patterns (Miller, 1981). As a child's communicative skills advance, both in terms of complexity and appropriateness, his utterances may be quantified according to a set of language functions that are based on the developmental stages of language acquisition.

By approximately three years of age, the child has entered what Halliday described as *Phase III* of adult language. This phase constitutes a multifunctional usage in expressive language. The child's speech functions in a variety of manners, including the following:

> ➤ Interpersonal — The utterance reflects an intention to interact with others.

> ➤ Textual — The utterance is based on previous utterances.

> ➤ Ideational and Experiential — The utterance is an attempt to express meaning.

The diagnostician may employ Halliday's seven basic functions of language to describe the child's language in terms of developmental sequence of acquisition, the constant reorganization of both form and function, and the development of multiple functions encountered with multiword utterances.

Prutting Pragmatic Protocol

The *Prutting Pragmatic Protocol* is a method of viewing how children aged five and older use language to signify conversational intent in a social setting (Prutting, 1983). It delineates the language used according to three major domains called *utterance acts*, *propositional acts*, and *illocutionary/perlocutionary acts* as either *appropriate* or *inappropriate*.

> Utterance Act — includes verbal, paralinguistic, and nonverbal aspects of language

> Propositional Act — involves semantics, word relationships, and stylistic variation in communication delivery

> Illocutionary/Perlocutionary Act — encompasses conversational skills such as topicalization and turn-taking

A raw score and a weighted score are acquired, allowing the diagnostician to establish a measure of severity.

Using these pragmatic instruments in a variety of settings offers the greatest degree of accuracy in assessing the social-pragmatic difficulties children with Asperger's Syndrome experience. Attention should be given to the child's ability to interact with others, especially same-aged peers. While classroom participation may offer insight, chances are that a greater degree of involvement (or lack thereof) may be found in unstructured school situations. Recess time and PE offer natural opportunities to investigate the child's ability to interact with other children. Here are some questions to think about during such observations:

> Does the child remain socially isolated?

> When children approach the child, does he show signs of anxiety?

> Is his participation in group games as competent as those of his peers?

> Are his motor skills as well developed as his peers' motor skills?

> Does he engage in imaginative play with his peers?

> Does he script rigid roles for others to adhere to?

Opportunities for observation may also be found in school performances, especially class plays and reenactments. The following page lists some helpful questions to guide such observations.

> ➢ Is role-playing especially difficult for the child?

> ➢ Can he take characters' perspectives to embellish their roles?

> ➢ Does he adequately project his voice such that his audience can hear him?

> ➢ Does he take turns appropriately?

Rating Scales and Profiles

While no definitive instrument is available to accurately assess the global aspects of Asperger's Syndrome, many different rating scales are available commercially. These scales may provide insight into the child's strengths and weaknesses.

Asperger Syndrome (and high-functioning autism) Diagnostic Interview (ASDI) (Gillberg et al., 2001)

The *ASDI* is a new instrument designed to determine the presence of Asperger's Syndrome by using interview questions. Preliminary data suggest positive results in both reliability and validity.

Australian Scale for Asperger's Syndrome
(Atwood, 1998)

This scale includes 24 items based on a set of diagnostic criteria. Each question is followed by an example for clarification. It is divided into five categories: social and emotional abilities (including communication skills), cognitive skills, specific interests, and movement skills. It is not standardized and employs terminology unique to Australian English, which may confuse some individuals.

Autism Diagnostic Interview—Revised
(Lord et al., 1994)

Developed as a research instrument for use with parents, it provides a standardized interview to elicit responses through open-ended questions designed to aid in the diagnosis of autism. Formal instruction is required prior to utilizing this instrument.

Autism Diagnostic Observation Schedule
(Lord et al., 1989)

By providing a series of activities, the *Autism Diagnostic Observation Schedule* allows for rating the child's ability to interact socially, use imagination, and explain feelings. As with the *Autism Diagnostic Interview,* formal instruction is required prior to utilizing this instrument.

Autism Spectrum Screening Questionnaire
(Ehlers et al., 1999)

Designed in Sweden for parents and teachers, this questionnaire employs a rating scale for 27 behaviors intended to assess the three primary domains of social interaction, communication skills, and restricted and repetitive behavior; and secondary domains of motor coordination and miscellaneous difficulties. It currently is the only instrument available that has been field tested and validated.

Checklist for Autism in Toddlers (CHAT)
(Baron-Cohen et al., 1992)

The *CHAT* is designed for screening possible autistic symptoms as early as 18 months of age. It combines parental reports with direct observation and is a reliable instrument for identifying autism within this young population. It is not a reliable instrument for identifying more subtle forms of autistic spectrum disorders such as Asperger's Syndrome.

Childhood Autism Rating Scale (Schopler et al., 1980)

This rating scale is based on data obtained by observing various aspects of autism categorized into 15 diagnostic areas.

Parent Interview for Autism (PIA)
(Stone and Hogan, 1993)

The *PIA* is a structured interview designed to gather diagnostic information from parents of young children with autism. It requires parents to rate the frequency of occurrence of specific behaviors.

Psychoeducational Profile (PEP-R)
(Schopler et al., 1990)

The *PEP-R* provides a profile of a child's distinctive learning patterns through a series of activities designed to assess the behaviors of autism.

Real Life Rating Scale (RLRS) (Freeman et al., 1986)

The *RLRS* measures changes in behavior present in individuals with autism over time. It relies on observation for data collection and rates the presence and frequency of specific behaviors of autism.

A diagnostician MUST make a careful, meticulous review of data acquired from a wide variety of sources in order to determine whether an individual has Asperger's Syndrome. Unfortunately, due to the unique nature of this syndrome, misdiagnosis is a common occurrence; many of the behaviors these individuals present with can lead to incorrect diagnostic labeling. The astute diagnostician must be prepared to fully review the data obtained and must consider all possible diagnostic labels.

 # Misdiagnosis

Due to the unique nature of Asperger's Syndrome, an appropriate diagnosis is frequently not made until a child is an adolescent. By this time, well-intentioned diagnosticians have provided many different diagnostic labels, including *autism*, *ADHD*, *learning disabled*, *communication delayed*, and *emotionally handicapped/behavior disordered*. One study reported that of 32 children determined to have Asperger's Syndrome, 92% were provided with other diagnoses or educational labels (Church et al., 2000). Well-intentioned school psychologists, primary care physicians, psychologists, and psychiatrists provided these labels based on the information available to them, as well as their experience with the population. Accurate diagnosis is highly impacted by the experience each diagnostician has with a variety of populations to diagnose. The more limited the population and experience, the greater the chance of misdiagnosis. Research has supported this hypothesis by comparing the diagnostic skills of school psychologists in rural and urban settings. Those practicing in the rural settings had a much greater difficulty in assessing high-functioning autism (including Asperger's Syndrome) and often mislabeled these students first as children with behavior disorders and then as children with mental handicaps (Spears et al., 2001).

The old saying *If all you have is a hammer, then everything looks like a nail* certainly applies to diagnosing individuals who have Asperger's Syndrome. It is all too easy to misdiagnose these individuals. They have often been referred to a specific diagnostician skilled in a particular field for the sole purpose of obtaining a label within that field. When the diagnostician reviews the background information and relates it to the child in front of her, it becomes easy to choose those features that support the diagnostic label of her field or specialty. Although such a label relates in some manner to the child's difficulty, it may not adequately address the entire spectrum of deficits associated with Asperger's Syndrome.

Many of these individuals who have been mislabeled have undergone countless hours of inappropriate treatment at substantial cost. Mental health providers must be alert to this danger within their field and recognize that if a chronic mentally-ill patient remains resistant to treatment, then it may be appropriate to reconsider the diagnosis as possible Asperger's Syndrome (Ryan, 1992). Researchers have begun to recognize this dilemma and have suggested that current diagnostic manuals may need to be revised. They cite the presence of comorbid conditions that may indicate fundamental deficits (Gillberg and Billstedt, 2000).

Differential Diagnosis

Table 2, pages 37 and 38, offers a comparison of the symptoms associated with Asperger's Syndrome to diagnoses with which it is often confused. The terminology for this table is defined below.

Table 2: Terminology Defined

age at diagnosis	age when diagnosis may be acquired
desire for social interaction	desire to interact with others for socially engaging situations
gender specific	tendency for diagnosis to be expressed in one gender over another
IQ	general cognitive and intelligence skills
language onset	language milestones
motor praxis	presence of motor problems, clumsiness, and apraxia not attributed to muscle weakness
obsessive interests	presence of obsessive-compulsive behaviors
regression of skills	The individual presents with a regression of previously acquired skills.
syntax and semantics	command of syntax and semantics
verbal skills	capacity for verbal communication

Table 2:
Comparison of Clinical Symptoms by Diagnosis

	IQ	Age at Diagnosis	Motor Praxis	Language Onset	Regression of Skills	Verbal Skills	Syntax & Semantics	Desire Social Interaction	Obsessive Interests	Gender Specific
ADHD	Normal	> 3 years	Absent*	Normal	No	Normal	Reduced abstract language	Normal interest	Absent	9:1 male/female
Asperger's Syndrome	Normal*	> 3 years	Present*	Normal*	No	Normal	Above average	High interest	Present	5:1 male/female
Autism	Wide range (PIQ>VIQ)	< 3 years	Generally normal	Delayed	No	50% acquire language	Limited	Poor interest	Absent	No
Bipolar Disorder	Wide range	> 10 years	Absent	Normal	No	Normal	Deficient semantics	Dependent upon manic or depressive phase	Present	More common in males
Childhood Disintegrative Disorder	Severe	3-4 years	Significant decline/deficit	Severely delayed	Yes	Significantly impaired	Absent	Poor interest	Present	More common in males
Generalized Anxiety Disorder	Wide range	Childhood and adolescence	Deficits related to increased muscle tension	Normal	No	Normal	Normal	Excessive worry impacts social domain	Present	55-60% female
Major Depressive Disorder	Wide range	Any age, average is mid-20s	Agitation	Normal	No	Normal	Normal	Withdrawn; increased irritability impacts social skills	Hand wringing	Female only

* Disagreement exists in published literature.

	IQ	Age at Diagnosis	Motor Praxis	Language Onset	Regression of Skills	Verbal Skills	Syntax & Semantics	Desire Social Interaction	Obsessive Interests	Gender Specific
Mixed Receptive-Expressive Language Disorder	Wide range	3 years	Absent	Delayed	No	Normal	Limited	High interest	Absent	No
Obsessive-Compulsive Disorder	Wide range	> 5 years	Absent	Normal	No	Normal	Normal	May be impacted by type of OCD	High presence	No
Oppositional-Defiant Disorder	Normal	> 8 years	Absent	Normal	No	Normal	Deficient semantics	Negativistic & defiant behavior	Absent	More common in males (especially before puberty)
PDD-NOS	Wide range (PIQ/VIQ)	< 3 years	Absent	Delayed	No	Limited	Limited	Poor interest	Present	No
Rett's Syndrome	Severe-profound	< 3 years	Severe	Delayed	Yes	Significantly impaired	Absent	Poor interest	Hand wringing	Female only
Schizophrenia	Wide range	Late teens to mid-30s	Poor coordination (often secondary to medication)	Normal	No	Disorganized speech, auditory hallucinations	Grammatical inconsistencies (disorganized, tangential, & incoherent)	Flat affect impacts social skills	Persecutory delusions	Slightly higher rates for men
Separation Anxiety Disorder	Normal	> 4 years	Absent	Normal	No	Normal	Normal	High interest, especially with family members	Absent	No
Tourette's Disorder	Normal	> 6 years	Motor and vocal tics	Normal	No	Normal	Normal	Normal interest	Present	2:1 male/female

Description of Specific Disorders

> ## Attention Deficit Disorder (ADD), Attention Deficit/ Hyperactivity Disorder (ADHD)

Problems in attention are a clinical feature of Asperger's Syndrome. Many individuals are initially referred for suspected attention deficit disorder, but individuals with true ADD do not exhibit the extreme social interaction and social communication deficits associated with Asperger's Syndrome. ADHD individuals may have a tendency to dominate a topic, but their deficit is related to impulse control and not a true social communication disorder. Individuals with ADD can adjust their behavior by "reading" the facial cues of others. Initially, they may require direct instruction in attending to these cues, but thereafter, these students can detect and use these cues as effective communication tools. Standardized intelligence testing of students with ADD/ ADHD appears to produce weaknesses on coding and arithmetic subtests while a student with Asperger's Syndrome generally demonstrates good verbal ability and weaknesses on object assembly and coding subtests (Ehlers et al., 1997).

> ## Autism

Asperger's Syndrome can be differentiated from high-functioning autism by the proficiency of language among individuals with Asperger's Syndrome. In general, individuals with high-functioning autism have poorer social, communication, and language skills. Their skill development is typically uneven. Perhaps the easiest means of differentiating Asperger's Syndrome from high-functioning autism is that people with Asperger's Syndrome often use a pedantic speaking style (Ghaziuddin and Gerstein, 1996). Psychometric testing evidences a higher verbal mental age for Asperger's Syndrome (Eisenmajer et al., 1996). Individuals with autism also demonstrate peaks on the Block Design subtest of the *WISC-R*, whereas individuals with Asperger's Syndrome show good verbal ability and weaknesses on the Object Assembly and Coding Subtests (Ehlers et al., 1997).

➤ Behavior Disorder

In general, high-functioning autism can be distinguished from behavior disorders by the presence of poorer social skills, reduced communication and language proficiency, and an uneven skill development in individuals with Asperger's Syndrome or autism (Asarnow et al., 1987). In addition, those identified as behavior disordered do not have the odd and perseverative interests, early language delays, and poor pragmatics seen in the high-functioning population with autism (Spears et al., 2001).

➤ Bipolar Disorder

Manic episodes associated with bipolar disorder do not present with the same manner of social interactive deficits associated with Asperger's Syndrome. Individuals with manic episodes of bipolar disorder frequently show a severe disregard for societal rules and have a complete lack of concern about the impact their behavior has on others. This symptomatology differs from Asperger's Syndrome in that the behaviors do not exhibit the long-standing social-skill deficits seen in individuals with Asperger's Syndrome.

➤ Childhood Disintegrative Disorder (CDD)

This disorder is extremely rare and is characterized by normal development until at least 24 months, at which time a rapid neurodevelopmental regression occurs with symptoms similar to autism. Regression may begin as late as ten years of age. CDD can be distinguished from Asperger's Syndrome and autism by the loss of previously normal language, social, play, or motor skills in CDD. Restricted and repetitive behaviors appear to be more severe than those in early-onset autism.

➤ Generalized Anxiety Disorder

Many children with Asperger's Syndrome appear to be overly anxious. Their constant concern about potentially incorrect responses and their extreme difficulty during social situations may initially appear as a possible anxiety disorder. Closer inspection,

though, reveals that the individual presents with other traits not generally seen in the anxious patient. These differences will be manifested in Asperger's Syndrome as problems with social interaction, narrow and restricted areas of interest, pedantic language, and nonverbal communication problems. The anxious patient does not typically present with deficits in these areas to the extent that a person with Asperger's Syndrome does.

➢ Language Disorder

According to both the *DSM-IV TR* and *ICD-10*, delayed language acquisition is not seen in Asperger's Syndrome, although research is now showing that the presence of a speech delay may not be adequate for distinguishing Asperger's Syndrome from general language delay (Mayes and Calhoun, 2001). Children with typical language delay, however, do not present with the degree of social deficits in the areas of interaction and communication that typifies Asperger's Syndrome.

➢ Major Depressive Disorder (MDD)

Severe psychosocial stressors, such as death or divorce, frequently are catalysts for major depressive disorders. These disorders can be differentiated from Asperger's Syndrome by the presence of normal social skills, including interaction and communication, prior to the onset of the depressive symptoms. Symptoms of long-standing social-skill deficits are more consistent with Asperger's Syndrome than with MDD.

➢ Obsessive-Compulsive Disorder (OCD)

Obsessive-compulsive traits are extremely common within the Asperger's Syndrome population. Care should be exercised when considering OCD as the primary diagnosis. While the issues related to obsessive interests may initially be explained through this diagnosis, it fails to consider the social deficits seen in those with Asperger's Syndrome and the presence of high-level abstract-language deficits. Research into the relationship between obsessive-compulsive disorder and autism has

shown that 20% of OCD subjects demonstrate traits of autism or Asperger's Syndrome (Bejerot et al., 2001). These authors further hypothesized that OCD is often related to high-functioning autism and Asperger's Syndrome.

➢ Oppositional-Defiant Disorder

Individuals with Asperger's Syndrome differ from individuals with conduct disorder in the social functioning domain, despite relatively good cognitive ability. They also present with higher levels of anxiety and obsessive disorders than individuals with oppositional-defiant disorder. Both groups are found to present with elevated depression, suicidal ideation, increased temper outbursts, and defiance (Green et al., 2000).

➢ Pervasive Developmental Disorder-Not Otherwise Specified (PDD-NOS)

This diagnostic entity is reserved for those cases in which some, but not all, of the diagnostic criteria for autism are met. It frequently is used when either insufficient or unreliable information is present or when the diagnostician is reluctant to use the term *autism*.

➢ Rett's Syndrome

Unlike autism, this neurodegenerative disorder is limited to girls. It can be differentiated from autism by the presence of stereotypic hand movements and a significant reduction in head circumference growth rate that eventually leads to microencephaly.

➢ Schizophrenia

Misdiagnosis for childhood-onset schizophrenia is common. The relative rarity of the disorder and the ambiguous criteria used in diagnosing it, allow for frequent errors in making an appropriate diagnosis (McKenna et al., 1994). Individuals with Asperger's

Syndrome also look less often at a speaker than normal or schizoid control subjects (Tantam et al., 1993). Deficits in nonverbal expression are associated with Asperger's Syndrome but not with personality disorder (Tantam, 1988). Other research has demonstrated that a differential diagnosis between psychotic children and high-functioning autism can be made on the basis of the child with high-functioning autism having poorer language and social skills, and extreme difficulty in adapting to change. These observations were supported by data obtained on the *Childhood Autism Rating Scale* and the *Real Life Rating Scale* (Matese et al., 1994). In general, the psychotic symptoms are often overemphasized when diagnosing Asperger's Syndrome, especially in an emergency psychiatric setting (Raja and Azzoni, 2001). Some researchers feel that longitudinal observation is the only means to accurately distinguish between schizophrenia and Asperger's Syndrome (Dauner and Martin, 1978).

Chapter 4:
Case History

Thomas is an eleven-year-old child who transferred to Abraham Lincoln Middle School in January of the present year. Previously he attended Holy Rosary Cathedral School, First Baptist Academy, and Lake Ivanhoe Preparatory School. Reports indicate he had extensive difficulty in the areas of socialization and behavior. He frequently failed to complete homework assignments and often was unmotivated and unresponsive to the school agenda. The school had frequent conferences with his parents in an attempt to effectuate a positive change. Thomas's behavior frequently necessitated numerous adaptations to the curriculum until such time that his school could no longer accommodate him. The school strongly recommended that Thomas transfer to another school.

Thomas's current teacher reports that he has significant difficulty in socialization. He has no friends and often attempts to dominate the conversation with persistent discussions about telephone poles. When redirected, he frequently engages in power struggles and often becomes defiant. He refuses to participate in class discussions and cannot concentrate during lectures. At these times, he often wanders around the classroom for no particular reason. He excels at factual material but has extreme difficulty with reasoning and relating current information to daily situations. His problem-solving skills are weak. Fine-motor skills are a concern because his written material is often illegible and missing crucial information. His classmates rarely ask him to participate in group activities and he eats his lunch in an isolated area in the cafeteria. Changes in class routines are extremely difficult for him.

Based on these concerns, a comprehensive evaluation was recommended. Results follow.

Chronological Age: 11.4

Social Services Evaluation

Thomas is the product of a full-term pregnancy. Prenatal history was unremarkable. Developmental milestones were appropriate for sitting, walking, and toilet training. Language development was somewhat slow with first words at approximately two years of age and phrases suddenly appearing at about three years of age. Some concern was expressed as he often appeared to be repeating previous conversations.

His father holds a Ph.D. in computer programming. He describes himself as a workaholic who takes pride in the fact that his father and brothers are engineers, architects, and computer wizards. His mother is a graphic artist for a local magazine. He has no siblings.

His parents describe him as a loner who does not want to associate with other children, but he is extremely affectionate at home to both parents. He delights in reading and appears to show an interest in computers.

Previous teachers report social skills to be a concern, especially during elementary school years. He has had a history of poor peer relations and few friendships. His academic progress was age appropriate, especially for factual information. He was reported to have difficulty with pencil and paper tasks. Thomas was obsessed with trains and could describe them in exquisite detail. Currently his interest is telephone poles and all spontaneous conversation revolves around telephone poles. It should be noted that during these "conversations," his speech becomes somewhat odd with a higher pitch and a sing-song quality. Previous attempts at accommodating his needs focused on modifying the academic requirements by using small-group instruction and reducing the demands for written material. He was often assigned peer buddies and given preferential seating, where specific instruction on reasoning skills was provided. Teachers continued to report minimal change and often sought assistance for appropriate management.

Psychological Services Evaluation

Wechsler Intelligence Scale for Children–III (Wechsler, 1991)

	Score	Highest Subtest	Lowest Subtest
Verbal Subtests	108	Similarities	Comprehension
Performance Subtests	96	Block Design	Coding
Full Scale IQ	103		

Woodcock Johnson–Revised: Tests of Achievement

(Woodcock et al., 2001)

	Age Equiv.	Grade Equiv.	Percentile Rank	Standard Score
Broad Reading	9.9	4.3	28	91
Letter-Word Identification	12.9	7.1	71	108
Reading Fluency*	8.9	3.4	14	84
Passage Comprehension	8.5	3.1	18	87
Broad Mathematics	11.6	6.0	54	102
Calculation	12.4	6.7	66	106
Math Fluency*	8.0	2.6	2	69
Applied Problems	13.0	7.6	73	109
Broad Written Language	9.7	4.4	27	91
Spelling	11.1	5.7	48	99
Writing Fluency*	9.0	3.6	10	81
Writing Sample	9.4	3.7	28	91

* impacted by issues related to anxiety and fine-motor deficits

Childhood Autism Rating Scales (Schopler et al., 1980)

Total Score: 27.5 (Nonautistic)

Speech-Language Evaluation

Expressive One-Word Picture Vocabulary Test–Revised

(Gardner, 1990)

Raw Score	93	Scaled Score	16
Age Equivalent	>11.11	Percentile Rank	96
Standard Score	126	Stanine	9

The Listening Test (Barrett et al., 1992)

	Raw Score	Age Equiv.	Percentile Rank	Standard Score
Main Idea	14	11.4	57	106
Details	12	9.2	35	97
Concepts	15	above norms	87	116
Reasoning	10	7.10	9	78
Story Comprehension	11	8.2	16	85
Total Test	62	9.10	29	96

Classroom Listening Scale: 2

The Language Processing Test *(Richard and Hanner, 1995)*

	Raw Score	Age Equiv.	Percentile Rank	Standard Score
Associations	10	8.8	34	97
Categorizations	10	6.8	6	71
Similarities	10	10.6	46	101
Differences	10	above norms	56	105
Multiple Meanings	9	8.7	15	86
Attributes	42	above norms	28	91
Total Test	91	above norms	7	76

Test of Word Knowledge (Wiig and Secord, 1991)

	Raw Score	Percentile Rank	Standard Score
Synonyms	34	84	13
Figurative Usage	12	9	6
Receptive Composite		42	97
Word Definitions	48	91	14
Multiple Contexts	19	75	12
Expressive Composite		87	117
Total Score		70	108
Age Equivalent: 11.11			
Expressive Vocabulary	25	91	91
Receptive Vocabulary	38	95	95
Word Opposites	36	95	95

Test of Problem Solving (Zachman et al., 1994)

	Raw Score	Age Equiv.	Percentile Rank	Standard Score
Total Test	63	10.0	24	93

Prutting Pragmatic Protocol (Prutting, 1983)

Raw Score: 23
Weighted Score: 41
Rating: Severe

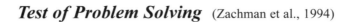

Diagnostic Process

Based on the initial reports provided to the diagnosticians, the following disorders were initially hypothesized to be contributing to Thomas's social and academic problems:

➢ Attention Deficit Disorder
➢ Autism, Behavior Disorder
➢ Bipolar Disorder
➢ Generalized Anxiety Disorder
➢ Language Disorder
➢ Major Depressive Disorder
➢ Obsessive-Compulsive Disorder
➢ Oppositional-Defiant Disorder
➢ PDD-NOS
➢ Schizophrenia

Someone had mentioned *Rett's Syndrome*, but this diagnosis was immediately dismissed as it is limited to girls. Thomas also did not present with *childhood disintegrative disorder (CDD)* because of his age and the long-standing problems for which this evaluation is taking place. Even if his problems only recently manifested, they would not be severe enough to constitute a consideration of CDD. Likewise, the diagnosis of *depression* was dismissed since Thomas presented with deficits typically not associated with this diagnosis; specifically, longstanding deficits in social skills. In addition, no particular stressor was identified as a precurser to a major depressive episode.

Autism and *PDD-NOS* were ruled out because the diagnostic features associated with them present with greater difficulties than those Thomas exhibited. This decision is supported by the low score Thomas obtained on the *Childhood Autism Rating Scale* and his relatively good language skills. Children with autism and PDD-NOS would typically present with greater social deficits than those Thomas exhibited. These children also do not exhibit the pedantic qualities seen in Thomas's language.

The presence of noncompliance, rage, and refusal to participate in academic activities do lend support for diagnoses of a *behavior disorder* (an academic label), *oppositional-defiant disorder*, and/or a *bipolar disorder* (manic episode). On the surface, these labels do appear appropriate. However, Thomas's longstanding history of social-skills deficits and significant pragmatic language disorder do not support the criteria for these diagnostic labels. Had the diagnostic process not provided input regarding Thomas's social and language functions, the criteria for these labels may have been rightfully considered.

Thomas's persistent need to dominate the conversational topic and his frequent, aimless wandering lend support for *attention deficit disorder (ADD)*. However, his inability to establish friendships and social-skills problems demonstrate different characteristics than those seen in ADD/ADHD. The deficits seen in this population typically are secondary to inappropriate impulse control. Thomas's deficits appear to be related to a larger problem with social skills. He has difficulty with intentionality and the communication required for social regulation. ADD/ADHD does not manifest itself in the same manner, so the use of this label as the primary handicapping situation would not be appropriate for Thomas.

Just as with the previous disorders, Thomas's behaviors do not fully support a diagnosis of *generalized anxiety disorder*. While he may have anxious moments, this label does not fully explain his behaviors that are not related to anxiety.

Obsessive-compulsive disorder (OCD) would appear to be appropriate. Thomas is obsessed with telephone poles, yet true *OCD* does not present with the high-level language deficits that Thomas has. In addition, his pragmatic language skills as measured by his performance on the *Prutting Pragmatic Protocol* do not support the diagnosis of *OCD*.

Schizophrenia does not appear to be an appropriate diagnosis. Thomas's background history and current functioning do not indicate any episodes of

hallucination. In addition, his difficulty with abstract language and his poor response to changes in routine are not features associated with schizophrenia.

Language disorder would appear to present a viable diagnostic label. Thomas does evidence deficits in the areas of abstract language comprehension and pragmatic language. When one views the diagnostic findings against the criteria for Asperger's Syndrome, however, it becomes apparent that a label of *language disorder* does not fully explain his problems.

If we use Table 1 to relate Thomas's current deficits and behaviors to the diagnosis of Asperger's Syndrome, we can see that this label is more appropriate for Thomas.

Table 1:
Comparison of Three Major Classification Systems for Asperger's Syndrome

➤ Findings for Thomas are presented in *italics*.

DSM-IV TR	ICD-10	Gillberg's Criteria
Qualitative impairment in social interaction (A)* *Significant difficulty with social skills reported*	Qualitative abnormalities in reciprocal social interaction (B)* *Significant difficulty with social skills reported*	Social impairment with extreme egocentricity (A)* *Significant difficulty with social skills reported*
Marked impairment in the use of multiple nonverbal behaviors such as eye-to-eye gaze, facial expression, body postures, and gestures to regulate social interaction (A1)* *Not reported*	Failure to adequately use eye-to-eye gaze, facial expression, body posture, and gesture to regulate social interaction (B1)* *Not reported*	Poor appreciation of social cues (A2)* *Does not recognize nonverbal language cues used by others*
Failure to develop peer relationships appropriate to developmental level (A2)* *Does not have friends*	Failure to develop (in a manner appropriate to mental age, despite ample opportunities) peer relationships that involve mutual sharing of interests, activities and emotions (B2)* *Does not have friends; peers shun him; dominates topic of conversation.*	Inability to interact with peers (A1)* *Peers often shun him.*

* Letters and numbers in parentheses in this table refer to the corresponding outline designations on pages 12-17. The *DSM-IV TR* column follows the original order of this information.

Table 1 , *continued*

DSM-IV TR	ICD-10	Gillberg's Criteria
A lack of spontaneous seeking to share enjoyment, interests, or achievements with other people (A3)* *Not directly reported but has difficulty with perspective taking*	Lack of spontaneous seeking to share enjoyment, interests, or achievements with other people (e.g., a lack of showing, bring-ing, or pointing out to other people objects of interest to the individual) (B4)* *Not directly reported but has difficulty with perspective taking*	
Lack of social or emotional reciprocity (A4)* *Dominates conversation; cannot sustain conversation; significant difficulty with perspective taking*	Lack of socio-emotional reciprocity as shown by an impairment or deviant response to other people's emotions; or lack of modulation of behavior according to social context; or a weak integration of social, emotional, and communicative behaviors (B3)* *Dominates conversation; cannot sustain conversation; significant difficulty with perspective taking*	Inappropriate social and emotional responses (A3)* *Dominates conversation; cannot sustain conversation; significant difficulty with perspective taking*
Restricted repetitive and stereotyped patterns of behavior, interests, and activities (B)* *Obsessed with telephone poles*	The individual exhibits an unusually intense, circum-scribed interest or restricted, repetitive and stereotyped patterns of behavior, interests, and activities. (C)* *Obsessed with telephone poles*	Limited interests and preoccupation (B)* *Obsessed with telephone poles* More rote than meaning (B1)* Repetitive adherence (B3)*

* Letters and numbers in parentheses in this table refer to the corresponding outline designations on pages 12-17. The *DSM-IV TR* column follows the original order of this information.

DSM-IV TR	*ICD-10*	Gillberg's Criteria
Encompassing preoccupation with one or more stereotyped and restricted patterns of interest that is abnormal either in intensity or focus (B1)*	An encompassing preoccupation with stereotyped and restricted patterns of interest that are abnormal in content or focus; or one or more interests that are abnormal in their intensity and circumscribed nature though not in the content or focus (C1)*	More rote than meaning (B1)*
Obsessed with telephone poles	*Obsessed with telephone poles*	*Obsessed with telephone poles* Exclusive of other interests (B2)*
Apparently inflexible adherence to specific, nonfunctional routines or rituals (B2)*	Apparently compulsive adherence to specific, nonfunctional routines or rituals (C2)*	Repetitive routines or rituals (C)* Imposed on self (C1)* Imposed on others (C2)*
Stereotyped and repetitive motor mannerisms (B3)*	Stereotyped and repetitive motor mannerisms that involve hand/finger flapping or twisting or complex whole-body movements (C3)*	
Persistent preoccupation with parts or objects (B4)*	Preoccupation with part-objects or non-functional elements of play materials (such as their color, the feel of their surface, or the noise/vibration that they generate) (C4)*	

* Letters and numbers in parentheses in this table refer to the corresponding outline designations on pages 12-17. The *DSM-IV TR* column follows the original order of this information.

Table 1 , *continued*

DSM-TR	ICD-10	Gillberg's Criteria
The disturbance causes clinically significant impairment in social, occupation, or other important areas of functioning. (C)* *Significant difficulty with socialization and establishing friendships*		Inappropriate social and emotional responses (A)* *Significant difficulty with socialization and establishing friendships*
There is no clinically significant delay in language (D)* *Language milestones fit this criteria.*	There is no clinically significant general delay in spoken or receptive language. Diagnosis requires that single words should have developed by 2 years of age or earlier and that communicative phrases be used by 3 years of age or earlier. (A)* *Language milestones fit this criteria.*	Delayed early language is possible. (D1)* Impaired comprehension, especially with literal and implied meanings (D4)* *Normal developmental process not exhibited. ". . . phrases suddenly appearing at about 3 years of age."*
There is no clinically significant delay in cognitive development or in the development of age-appropriate self-help skills, adaptive behavior (other than in social interaction), and curiosity about the environment in childhood. (E)* *Full Scale IQ=103*	There is no clinically significant general delay in cognitive development. Self-help skills, adaptive behavior, and curiosity about the environment during the first 3 years should be at a level consistent with normal intellectual development. (A)* *Full Scale IQ=103*	Impaired comprehension, especially with literal and implied meanings (D4)* *Supported by performance on The Listening Test and Test of Word Knowledge (Figurative Usage subtest)*

* Letters and numbers in parentheses in this table refer to the corresponding outline designations on pages 12-17. The *DSM-IV TR* column follows the original order of this information.

DSM-TR	ICD-10	Gillberg's Criteria
Criteria not met for another specific Pervasive Development Disorder or Schizophrenia (F)*	The disorder is not attributable to the other varieties of pervasive developmental disorder: simple schizophrenia, schizotypal disorder, obsessive-compulsive disorder, anankastic personality disorder, reactive and disinhibited attachment disorders of childhood. (D)*	
	Motor milestones may be somewhat delayed and motor clumsiness is usual, although not a necessary diagnostic feature. (A)* *Fine-motor issues present*	Motor clumsiness may not always be seen. (F)* *Fine-motor issues present*
		Speech and language peculiarities (D)* *Excellent rote skills, poorer on tasks requiring reasoning and problem solving* Superficially perfect expressive language (D2)* *Pedantic quality* Odd prosody, peculiar voice (D3)* ". . . Speech becomes somewhat odd with a higher pitch and somewhat of a sing-song quality."

* Letters and numbers in parentheses in this table refer to the corresponding outline designations on pages 12-17. The *DSM-IV TR* column follows the original order of this information.

Table 1 , *continued*

DSM-TR	*ICD-10*	Gillberg's Criteria
		Nonverbal communication problems (E)
		Limited use of gestures (E1)
		Clumsy body language (E2)
		Inappropriate facial expression (E3)
		Difficulty with physical proximity (E4)
Reprinted with permission from the *Diagnostic and Statistical Manual of Mental Disorders, Fourth Edition, Text Revision.* Copyright 2000 American Psychiatric Association.	Reprinted with permission from the *Tenth Revision of the International Classification of Disease*, Geneva, World Health Organization, 1989.	Gillberg and Gillberg, 1989

* Letters and numbers in parentheses in this table refer to the corresponding outline designations on pages 12-17. The *DSM-IV TR* column follows the original order of this information.

Based on an analysis of his performance against the criteria for *Asperger's Syndrome*, it becomes apparent that this diagnostic label is more appropriate for Thomas than other labels.

Chapter 5:
Theory of Mind

The term *Theory of Mind* has been used to describe the cognitive processes inherent in interpersonal actions. It specifically concerns itself with an individual's ability to think about what another individual may be thinking and his ability to act upon it. Such actions may be influenced according to the information obtained through not only the individual's mental state but of another's mental state as well. In short, it is the ability to know what you are thinking about, what I am thinking about, and that I know you are thinking about it, too.

As confusing as this may seem, it is very simple in nature. When a child looks at a teacher and then points to an object on a shelf while looking at it, and then glances back at the teacher, he is nonverbally stating, "See that thing over there? I want you to get it for me." No words were used, but the message was effectively communicated. The child knew that the teacher would recognize what he wanted and would act upon it accordingly. This skill is an important aspect in the concept of Theory of Mind.

> *"No words were used, but the message was effectively communicated."*

When a child with autism grabs a teacher's arm and uses it as an extension of his own to obtain the desired toy on the shelf, he is not demonstrating the concept of Theory of Mind. The teacher's arm became a tool for the child and could easily have been substituted with a child's toy, similar to the robotic claw arm activated by a squeeze grip. It was simply an extension of his own arm. The child did not attempt to communicate a message to the teacher. Rather, he utilized the teacher as a means to an end. Had he demonstrated some degree of reciprocal interaction that basically communicated his desired intent, then he would have demonstrated a rudimentary form of Theory of Mind.

Another example is when a child quickly looks at his neighbor's test and then at his teacher. The teacher, having observed the entire scene, glares back at the child. The child now rethinks his original intention of obtaining a few answers from his neighbor, knowing that his teacher realizes what he is up to.

The essence behind the Theory of Mind is the ability to determine what another person is thinking, and further knowing that the other person knows what you are thinking. For many children within the autism spectrum, of which Asperger's is a part, this concept is extremely difficult to grasp. It is this faulty information processing that some contend contributes to the deficient communication skills seen in this population.

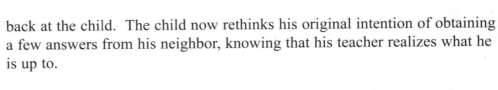

"...Theory of Mind is the ability to determine what another person is thinking, and further knowing that the other person knows what you are thinking."

To test this theory, Simon Baron-Cohen (Baron-Cohen et al., 1985) developed "The Sally/Anne Test" in which the performance of children with autism was compared to a group of children with Down Syndrome and normally developing four-year-old children. All subjects possessed mental ages in excess of four years. A scenario was acted out in front of all the subjects using two dolls named Sally and Anne. Sally had a basket and Anne had a box. Sally goes for a walk after having placed a marble in her basket while Anne was watching. While Sally is out walking, Anne removes the marble from Sally's basket. She places it in her box and waits for Sally to return. When Sally returns, she decides to play with her marble. At this point, the examiner turns to each child and asks, "Where will Sally look for her marble?" The correct response is "in the basket," as that is where Sally placed it before leaving for her walk. She could not possibly have known that Anne removed it. This correct response was provided by both the normally developing children and the children with Down Syndrome. In contrast, the children with autism consistently responded, "In the box." They failed to take on Sally's perspective and, consequently, responded incorrectly.

Children who cannot take on another individual's perspective invariably have significant difficulties in social communication skills. They become blinded by their inability to view the world in any other manner than their own. Is it any wonder these children are viewed as egocentric?

Children who have difficulty taking others' perspectives also have difficulty relating information appropriately to others. Frequently they begin conversations in mid-thought. It is as if they assume everyone else is thinking exactly as they are. To these children, the human brain is networked together just as computers are.

The *Star Trek* movies have a wonderful example of this concept of networked cognitive wiring. In these movies, there is a race of evil alien beings that are part man and part machine, known as the Borg. While each individual being is capable of functioning independently, they all belong to a "collective." The interesting thing about these individuals is that each one is capable of monitoring the thoughts of every other individual within the collective, no matter how far apart they are. They have no need for direct communication because each individual is capable of recognizing the thoughts of its associates.

Unlike the Borg, humans do not have the luxury of telepathic thought. Instead, we must rely on some form of active communication to interact with our associates. Speech, the quickest and easiest method, continues to require dynamic participation by both the speaker and the listener. A failure of one party to fully and completely incorporate the other into the message will invariably lead to a breakdown in communicative effectiveness.

Children with Asperger's Syndrome typically have extreme difficulty taking others' perspectives and, consequently, fail to communicate adequately. For many children, this difficulty leads to specific, odd mannerisms that often are equally puzzling to themselves and to others.

Not being able to fully recognize someone else's intention is an extremely frustrating liability. A teacher may easily admonish a child if the response to his question "Do you have the time?" is "Yes." Few students respond in such a manner. They would quickly recognize the teacher's true intent and offer the correct time. Unfortunately, the child with Asperger's Syndrome fails to recognize the intent behind the teacher's question and responds to the question literally; hence the incorrect answer. To him, his response to the teacher's question was an appropriate one. Not capable of recognizing his error, he becomes confused when the teacher expresses irritation with his response.

Ulterior motives are extremely difficult for children with Asperger's Syndrome to recognize. Again, the concept of Theory of Mind is directly related to their ineffective skills. They do not recognize the manipulation

being performed on them and invariably respond inappropriately. How many times have we seen a child perform foolish activities to impress his peers, not recognizing that they are actually laughing *at* him and not *with* him? Children with Asperger's Syndrome frequently are unable to recognize the mean spirit behind a prankster's request and naively follow through with it. When problems result, they are incapable of recognizing their mistake.

Returning to the example of Thomas, the telephone pole expert, this child could not comprehend the fact that his fascination with telephone poles was not universally enjoyed. As a result, he was overbearing to the point of being boring. He failed to recognize the cues in others and therefore could not be expected to show the slightest concern with his listener's lack of interest.

"…this child could not comprehend the fact that his fascination with telephone poles was not universally enjoyed."

Each of these instances demonstrates in some manner the impact perspective taking plays in our daily lives. Theory of the Mind attempts to describe these difficulties so that patterns of deficient processing may be addressed more adequately. Each deficient area associated with the concept of Theory of Mind is intricately woven within the social fabric of society. A failure to adequately master any or all of these skills will be painfully obvious to all — except the child with Asperger's Syndrome.

Chapter 6:
Social & Emotional Issues

 ## Skills & Deficits

Social Interaction

Perhaps the greatest area of difficulty for the child with Asperger's Syndrome is within the domain of social interaction. A young child with Asperger's Syndrome trying to play with a group of his classmates is guaranteed to produce a variety of issues that will cause bewilderment, alarm, and even anger. In his attempt to engage his friends, he will use a variety of skills he has learned over the years. Unfortunately for him, his peers will probably not appreciate these skills. Because taking someone else's perspective is extremely difficult for him, he will often fail to perceive the interests and desires of his classmates. They quickly recognize his difference in this area and, being children, they will not tolerate his social ineptness. The result for the child with Asperger's Syndrome is further isolation and continued feelings of rejection.

Unlike a child with classical autism, a child with Asperger's Syndrome desires social interaction. He attempts to engage others but frequently uses socially inappropriate means to interact with others. The response he obtains is often not what he desired. Cognitively, he is capable of recognizing his dilemma. He desires friendships but cannot understand why he is taken advantage of or shunned. He realizes something must be done, but he is unable to utilize the appropriate techniques that society takes for granted. This inability increases his anxiety in social settings.

Social Rules

It is the unwritten rules of social interaction that cause the child with Asperger's Syndrome to experience significant distress. He cannot relate to the concept of "fuzzy logic." As a result, he has an extremely difficult time with the "gray" areas of social rules. To the child with Asperger's Syndrome, rules require conformity. They are rigid, unyielding entities demanding everyone's strict adherence. They do not allow for shades of gray and exist in only two colors, white and black. There is zero tolerance for diversity or interpretation.

If only social interaction were that easy! The reality is that social rules are not rigid. They continuously change and are based on the demands of the situation, people, and environment. What works well with one individual is a recipe for disaster with another. And children, being children, have not as yet acquired the capability to handle errors in social interaction in a manner that does not heap excessive anxiety on the offending child. The typical way a child handles such problems is by ridiculing or shunning the offender and pointing out the problem to anyone who will listen, usually in a loud voice.

Adults, however, are oftentimes more accepting of social errors. They may not appreciate them, but they will most likely react in a manner that is easier for the offender to accept. They may glance at the child and then at the parent, intimating that the parent is ultimately responsible for the child's difficulty. The social rule structure among adults is generally more established and allows the child to predict the outcome more easily. Children, unlike adults, do not react to social errors in the same way. As a result, many children with Asperger's Syndrome prefer to interact with adults rather than peers.

By approximately the early elementary school years, children with Asperger's Syndrome have discernible differences from their same-aged peers in the social domain. Cognitively, they realize they are different from their peers, but they cannot produce a positive change based on their perception of the difference. At about this time, they may develop their own compensatory strategies to deal with their social ineptness. They may become more introverted and adopt a quiet, unassuming manner to help them mask their inefficiencies, or they may develop a more active, animated style of interaction that transgresses even more social rules. Either of these inept strategies further alienates children with Asperger's Syndrome from their peers.

Gullibility

Being different sets these children up for ridicule and practical jokes. In their desire to make friends, they often fail to use appropriate judgment and naively follow through with peer requests, no matter how bizarre. It is not uncommon for a student with Asperger's Syndrome to approach a teacher and say something grossly rude or obscene. Shocked by this flagrant transgression, the teacher summarily punishes the student for his insolence. But did the child intend to create such furor? Did he truly desire to infuriate his teacher to earn her wrath? Probably not.

It is crucial that teachers recognize this trait of gullibility and consider the possibility that the child was set up purposefully to create a scene. The wise teacher will recognize this possibility and ask the student what happened in an attempt to identify the instigator of the event.

Egocentricity

Many children with Asperger's Syndrome are described as "egocentric." The demands they place on their peers in play activities are extreme. It is not uncommon to watch them script out an entire routine prior to engaging in play activities. Each child is summarily assigned a role to play with no concern evidenced for his interest or desire. Transgressions in this assigned script are forcefully prohibited. To many observers, this behavior appears egocentric.

As previously described, children with Asperger's Syndrome have extreme difficulty recognizing someone else's perspective. They fail to perceive the nonverbal cues individuals use to indicate boredom, displeasure, and disgust. While other individuals recognize

these messages, the child with Asperger's Syndrome does not. He continues his discussion on the most mundane or morbid topics without regard to his listener. In effect, he shows a complete lack of awareness of others' emotions and interests. This ignorance, too, creates the impression of egocentricity.

It is hard to establish friendships when everyone views you as egocentric and inflexible. Few individuals delight in being perceived as subservient. Because of their rigidity, many children with Asperger's Syndrome have an extremely difficult time initiating and sustaining friendships.

Perhaps one of the most common traits of individuals with Asperger's Syndrome is the tendency to talk *at* people and not *to* people. Thomas, the child previously described who fixated on telephone poles, is a classic example. Despite abundant cues, he was incapable of recognizing his listener's complete lack of interest. Thomas continued with his insatiable interest in telephone poles and assumed everyone else held a similar interest. This pattern of speech is described as *pedantic* in that the person is talking incessantly but not truly conversing. Children with Asperger's Syndrome have even been described as "Little professors who can't understand social cues" (O'Neil, 1999).

This penchant for long monologues quickly becomes tiresome for many listeners and further serves to alienate children with Asperger's Syndrome from their peers. Some researchers (Ghaziuddin and Gerstein, 1996) have even postulated that this pedantic speaking style is unique to Asperger's and may be useful in differentiating it from high-functioning PDD.

Perhaps what creates this difficulty for individuals with Asperger's Syndrome is their inability to relate to their listeners. Deficiencies associated with the Theory of Mind do not allow them to understand their listeners' perspectives. As a result, they fail to use adequate turn taking and cannot recognize and respond to such nonverbal cues as facial expressions or rolling of the eyes. This lack of recognition would account for the intense, one-sided nature of their conversations. It would also account for their inability to recognize implied meanings.

Literal Interpretation of Messages

The simple phrase "Get out of here" can have two extremely different meanings. On the surface, it is a simple request to leave. However, in casual conversation, it is frequently said with a sarcastic drawl that completely changes the intended meaning. Instead of being a request to leave, it now means "I don't believe you."

Extremely literal interpretation of messages creates serious difficulties for students with Asperger's Syndrome. A teacher who responds with a similar sarcastic statement to such a student should not be bewildered when he suddenly rises from his chair and leaves the room. After all, he did exactly what his teacher asked him to do.

This inability to decipher implied meanings also extends to jokes and metaphors. Jokes are frequently based on implied meanings, double entendres, and exaggerations of fact. Individuals who are extremely literal miss the humor behind such statements. Metaphors are also confusing. To the child with Asperger's Syndrome, it is totally bewildering to look outside and see only rain when one is expecting "cats and dogs."

Prosodic Information

Social communication is also impacted by the degree of prosody attached to the message. The adeptness with which a speaker modulates her voice through inflection, stress, and pitch impacts the listener's desire to continue listening. The political speech delivered by a long-winded, monotone speaker is a classic example of the impact insufficient prosody has on listeners. Deficits in the use of prosody will cause not only listener boredom, but confusion as well. For many individuals with Asperger's Syndrome, the ability to modulate a vocal message through such prosodic features is a very difficult concept to understand. Recognizing prosody's role in communication is a challenge for those with Asperger's Syndrome. They simply do not attend to the subtle differences required for prosodic change.

The ability to recognize and describe the prosodic differences used by speakers of various forms of English is an example of the impact of prosodic differences among these speakers. The syntactic structure may remain the same for speakers of American English, British English, Australian English, and Indian English, but the prosodic features employed by each speaker are by no means similar. This ability to perceive and produce prosodic stress is extremely weak for individuals with Asperger's Syndrome.

English is a unique language in that appropriate use of prosodic stress can fundamentally alter a message's intent. For some individuals attempting to learn English as a second language, this remains a very difficult area to master. The statement "Please sit down" can take on a variety of meanings, from a polite request to a harsh demand, simply by the degree of prosodic stress placed on various words. For the individual with Asperger's Syndrome, understanding and using appropriate prosody is a constant struggle.

A prime example is someone who speaks loudly in areas where whispers are preferred. He may not realize how his elevated volume negatively impacts his companions due to his deficient perspective taking. Despite the glances from others, he continues without change, only to eventually get in trouble.

Some children with Asperger's Syndrome speak with inappropriate inflection, as if constantly asking questions. For these children, faulty prosodic skills cause extensive negative attention. Not being able to master the subtle differences required in prosody is yet another source of stress for these individuals.

Lack of Tact

Not knowing how to act among others presents another social dilemma for the individual with Asperger's Syndrome. How many times have we done something that caused us extensive embarrassment? However humiliated we were, our worst situation probably pales in comparison to the social predicaments individuals with Asperger's Syndrome experience repeatedly.

Here's a case in point. A child was leaving a speech-language pathologist's office and, to the horror of everyone in the room, blurted out, "You're fat!" while pointing to the next child's mother. Highly offended, the woman quickly lectured him on rudeness. What she didn't realize was that he wasn't being rude intentionally. He simply lacked tact and stated what to him was an obvious fact, for she was truly quite overweight.

How interesting the world would be if everyone actually did express what he was thinking! Society could be much more open and potential opportunities for social errors would be diminished. However, the frequency of assaults would probably increase significantly as we vented our anger at the constant criticism we received.

Teachers should be keenly aware of this unique directness trait among children with Asperger's Syndrome, as these students will undoubtedly say a variety of things capable of making a construction worker blush and do so while smiling broadly. An astute teacher will recognize that no matter how disturbing the comment, chances are exceedingly high that the child was not attempting to be rude. Rather, the child had no idea that a comment of such a nature could cause so much social distress.

Proxemics

The ability of children with Asperger's Syndrome to create social distress is also manifested in their poor understanding of the unwritten rules of social distance known as *proxemics*. While there is no standard as to what constitutes an appropriate distance one must keep between himself and his listener, an error of judgment in this area can quickly elevate the listener's anxiety level. It is not uncommon to see an individual with Asperger's Syndrome invade the personal space of his listener and be completely oblivious to how this behavior impacts his interaction. Likewise, a student with Asperger's Syndrome may carry on a conversation from a wide distance with the same vigor as if standing in front of the listener. Whether the speaker uses too little or too much distance between himself and his listener, the effect of both errors in proxemics is similar. It bewilders the listener and adds anxiety to the situation.

Conversation

The inability to initiate and sustain conversation also sets individuals with Asperger's Syndrome apart from society. Not knowing how to initiate a conversation is a hallmark for these individuals. For example, a librarian sees a child approaching and assumes he needs assistance in locating a specific book. Instead of the expected request, the student delivers a detailed analysis of telephone poles. Patiently waiting for his question, the librarian at first is amazed at his wealth of information, but she quickly realizes he is not about to stop. Social rules prevent her from simply walking away, so she attempts to interrupt him to determine the reason for his contact, only to be ignored. We can only begin to imagine what the librarian is thinking. Obviously, a litany on a current obsessive interest is not an efficient means of initiating a conversation.

Some individuals with Asperger's Syndrome may attempt to initiate conversation without the benefit of background information and completely bewilder their listeners. The uncanny ability to completely disregard a listener's needs by failing to provide a common referent or a suitable starting point further impedes these students' ability to establish appropriate social interaction.

When a speaker in a conversation realizes he has made a communication error, he often revises or paraphrases the message to make sure the listener understands the message. This ability to correct errors during conversations is called *conversational repair* and is another skill difficult for an individual with Asperger's Syndrome to master. When conversing, such a speaker may occasionally recognize making a communication error or sense the listener's confusion, but instead of trying to paraphrase or clarify the message, the speaker may signal the dilemma by employing a prolonged pause. To the listener, such a pause is a signal to change the topic. Typically, a speaker with Asperger's Syndrome pauses frequently enough that the topic is eventually manipulated to the person's obsessive interest. At this point, no more pauses occur because the person is now on familiar ground and can effectively control the conversation.

Inappropriate Behavior

Impaired social interaction among individuals with Asperger's Syndrome is also manifested by an uncanny ability to be taken advantage of by people who find delight in mistreating and disparaging others. It is not uncommon for a child with Asperger's Syndrome to perform some objectionable act and, when questioned why she would do such a thing, respond that a particular child told her to do so. The inability to determine the appropriateness of a request appears to be the reason for this deficit.

Some individuals with Asperger's Syndrome, in their zeal to obtain friends, attempt to buy friendship. They have been known to give away brand new tape players, Game Boys™, even clothing, in a futile effort to establish friends. Unfortunately, once the items have been handed over, the promise of friendship disappears.

This trait and the other traits previously described all have a common denominator. They serve to alienate these individuals from society by creating a global impairment in their ability to maintain appropriate social interaction.

Sensory Integration

Individuals with Asperger's Syndrome may also experience sensory difficulties typically not experienced by the general population. These sensory processing difficulties, known as *sensory integration problems*, may be related to either a hyper- or hypo-sensitivity issue. Research into the sensory-processing patterns of children with and without Asperger's Syndrome has shown significant differences in the sensory-processing patterns of children with Asperger's Syndrome as compared to their non-disabled peers (Dunn et al., 2002). The general population typically pays little attention to sensory issues unless they cross the threshold of intolerance. If a child has a faulty sensory system, however, this tolerance threshold may be at a different level. The child may then produce different behaviors from those we see in children without sensory-processing difficulties.

It is hard to engage in social activities if you dislike physical contact. Group activities are extremely difficult if you cannot tolerate touch. Situations that we generally think nothing about, such as shopping in a crowded mall or changing classes in school, may produce extreme anxiety if a person is hypersensitive to touch.

Consistency and Conformity

Despite having an IQ at or above normal values, individuals with Asperger's Syndrome have a restricted range of emotional resources available to deal with daily difficulties. The social demands placed on everyone change with each person we meet and each place we visit. To the individual with Asperger's Syndrome, these demands present extreme challenges requiring skills society takes for granted, but which these individuals have not as yet mastered. How, then, do they attempt to participate in a world full of unpredictability and change? By attempting to create a sense of conformity through continuity and sameness, just as those around them do.

Most of us have conformity in our use of language, dress, hairstyle, and numerous other aspects of daily life. We speak using the same level of language complexity as those around us. We dress according to predetermined patterns of expectation — casual, work, formal, or semi-formal. We style our hair in a manner that does not attract undue attention. All these domains are designed to enhance our appearance to others, both visually and psychologically.

We expect conformity in our environment as well. Neighborhoods tend to be homogenous. The unkempt yard stands apart from the others. When attending a professional conference, we expect a customary room layout. Large pillows on the floor and incense burning are not expected at such a conference.

We also expect conformity for behavior. When someone fails to conform to societal expectations, other people often point fingers, stare, or whisper about the person. Many individuals do not desire this negative attention and cringe when they unintentionally cause themselves to stand out from the crowd. Others, however, delight in this attention and readily seek it. Excessiveness invites attention.

Tattoos, facial body piercing, unusual fingernail length or decoration, and bizarre hair color serve as beacons for attention and supply a wealth of fodder for endless conversations.

Being able to predict what to expect is comforting. Not knowing what lies ahead is anxiety producing. In some cases, we deliberately expose ourselves to the unknown. The thrills associated with the amusement park fun house or haunted mansion would not exist if we knew beforehand what to expect. It is the heightened sense of the unknown that allows us to enjoy these settings.

But what if every day were like a walk through a fun house? The constant anxiety would no longer be enjoyable. Anxiety would quickly give way to dread as we attempted to make sense of the world around us. Our attempts at conformity would only serve to heighten our differences and further our feelings of ineptitude. Such is the world of those with Asperger's Syndrome.

Robert is in math class. His teacher is conducting a lesson on basic multiplication when, all of a sudden, Robert begins to fidget excessively. The teacher glances at him in an attempt to quiet him down. Robert is oblivious to the teacher's gaze and continues his fidgeting. He begins to repeatedly ask the same questions, disrupting the entire class. The teacher, now quite agitated, admonishes him in front of the class. As can be expected, the effect is disastrous. Robert is now embroiled in an emotionally charged battle of words with the teacher. The outcome for the class looks bleak.

Karen is showing signs of anxiety. She knows that a school assembly is scheduled later that day. She paces back and forth and refuses to enter her classroom, stating that her "feet don't work." Teachers vainly lecture to her about remaining in the hall after the bell rings. She doesn't budge.

George is having difficulty entering his bus for the ride home. He has noticed the bus driver is not his usual driver. When informed that his usual driver became ill earlier that day and this driver is a substitute, George continues to experience extreme anxiety.

The examples on the previous page are all symptoms of a similar need for consistency experienced by many children with Asperger's Syndrome. Even the slightest change is frequently a catalyst for excessive anxiety. Already burdened by a difficulty in interpreting the world around them, children with Asperger's Syndrome are overwhelmed by change.

The cases on page 71 exemplify the difficulties children with Asperger's Syndrome encounter in managing change. In most cases, it's easy to determine the sources of the children's difficulties. Robert's case is more difficult to determine. He continues to have a problem with the language of math. He cannot rapidly shift between the two terms *multiply* and *times*. His anxiety begins to mount because he cannot spontaneously request clarification.

A common feature among children diagnosed with Asperger's Syndrome is their need for constancy. This trait directly relates to their difficulty in interpreting the world around them. They have an extremely complicated time in the social domain. Two factors create extensive stress for these children: their inability to use social skills effectively themselves and their inability to accurately interpret the social responses of others. Not knowing what to expect can be highly unnerving for children with Asperger's Syndrome. Is it any wonder these children desire to establish a sense of consistency?

Environmental stress also increases anxiety. Physical proximity, noise, new faces, requests to participate, and sensations from clothing are just some of the things most children take in stride. For children with Asperger's Syndrome, these all contribute to increase the degree of anxiety they experience. It is no wonder these children tend to develop rituals, often including the following:

➢ Toys, games, and puppets must be played with according to a scripted routine. Deviations are not tolerated.

➢ Board games and group activities must be consistent and cannot accommodate cheating or improvised rules.

To children with Asperger's Syndrome, these demands are a means of assuring consistency and predictability. To their peers, they are demanding, overbearing behaviors.

While a young child's excessive rituals may seem simply eccentric, as the child ages, his peers will become less tolerant of this behavior. Disputes develop between the child and his peers, causing more stress that only intensifies his need for consistency. Children with Asperger's Syndrome find life much easier to predict when things are consistent. Some of these children may insist on using only a specific plate or drinking cup. Others may demand a specific television show or to have the same parent put them to bed every night. These rituals may not seem extreme, but if they are fostered, they may eventually dominate daily life and impact others' activities as well. At that point, society views such rituals as obsessive and extremely atypical. Some of these children have now crossed the boundary toward the beginnings of an obsessive-compulsive disorder.

Facing the Unknown

Not knowing what to expect is highly discomforting. We have all sensed a degree of trepidation associated with facing the unknown. Walking down a deserted street in the dark in a strange part of town, being suddenly called to the boss's office, and the first day at a new employment setting are all anxiety-producing situations. Each unknown situation creates a certain degree of stress. The mind begins to race through a variety of scenarios, each of which is designed to provide us with options to assist in interpreting the unknown.

But what if we were incapable of guessing what lies ahead? What if we couldn't think of options to ease our fear of the unknown? What if every day presented challenges that caused an untold degree of stress? Would we behave in the same manner as we currently do? Probably not.

Children with Asperger's Syndrome tend to worry excessively when they do not know what to expect. New classrooms, substitute teachers, changes in the seating assignment, pop quizzes, pep rallies, etc., may be viewed as inconveniences or cause for joy for many non-disordered students, but for children with Asperger's Syndrome, such situations create increased opportunities for uneasiness. These children's apprehension escalates far beyond that seen in the typical population. Unfortunately for these children, many people fail to recognize this trait and fail to offer opportunities for comfort. This insensitivity furthers these children's distress and increases their anxiety.

In addition to these difficulties, children with Asperger's Syndrome often experience sensory overload to a greater degree than non-disordered children. Lunchrooms, auditoriums, gymnasiums, and crowded hallways are usually loud with poor acoustic qualities. To normal children, these areas offer endless opportunities for random conversations with their friends — places where academic demands are minimal. These same places, however, are problematic for children with heightened sensory systems. The sounds, sights, and smells change constantly, and children with Asperger's Syndrome have little ability to create uniformity. They can't use the routines they previously relied upon. The degree of comfort needed to reduce the stress generated in these situations increases exponentially. The result is too often an unfavorable situation for everyone.

Rigidity: An Ineffective Coping Strategy

Coping skills for social and school situations do not come easily to children with Asperger's Syndrome. Their need for uniformity and the difficulties associated with social demands create situations requiring skills and talents that society generally takes for granted. Most children don't require specific training for social situations; they learn through personal experience and by example. Children with Asperger's Syndrome, in contrast, must be taught social skills very specifically. Then they need to practice these skills until they master them.

Social interactions regularly produce difficulties for children with Asperger's Syndrome. How, then, do they attempt to control these social situations so as to avoid such problems? By being an expert on a particular topic, regardless of what the topic is. The more knowledge one has on the topic, the safer the conversation. To the individual with Asperger's Syndrome, this trait is a self-learned technique for managing social interactions. To the general public, it is extremely odd, demanding behavior and yet another characteristic that separates an individual with Asperger's Syndrome from the rest of society.

This tendency toward intense fixations is a classic hallmark defining individuals with Asperger's Syndrome. It is not uncommon for these individuals to focus on the most mundane topic with an intensity unknown in any other population. Telephone poles, windmills, air-conditioning grates, surfboards, trains, bridges, and Glade Plug-Ins™ are just some of the areas of interest that have been reported. If given the opportunity, these children will latch onto unsuspecting individuals and provide them with every possible detail related to their obsessive interests. It is as if they have memorized an entire encyclopedia of facts about particular topics and are determined to provide listeners with every detail. Despite numerous attempts at redirecting them toward something more socially appropriate, they invariably manage to continue their lectures without regard to their listeners' interests.

By perseverating on their unique areas of interest, these individuals create a sense of continuity in what they perceive as a world full of uncertainties and doubt. When you are unsure how to behave in a situation or conversation, it is easier to control it yourself rather than let others control it for you. Doing so creates consistency instead of chaos; comfort instead of anxiety. This self-protective tendency to remain rigid limits these children's participation in what society considers as normal activities.

For teachers, such rigidity among children with Asperger's Syndrome creates unique problems within the academic curriculum. Despite every attempt at redirecting these students' attention to the current lesson, they often refuse to learn outside their areas of interest. It is extremely difficult for a teacher to conduct a lesson on ancient Greece or the industrial revolution when students are only concerned about telephone poles, windmills, air-conditioning grates, trains, bridges, surfboards, and/or Glade Plug-Ins™. Students with Asperger's Syndrome have a tendency to follow their own agendas, and these agendas invariably are not associated with the academic curriculum. More importantly, these students do not see the need to conform and/or participate in such lessons. The academic curriculum is of absolutely no interest to them.

This restricted range of interest produces a tendency to perseverate on specific questions. To the teacher, this feature is an extremely irritating trait and the sooner it is eliminated, the better for all. However, for the child, the persistent barrage of questions pertain-ing to a specific area of interest is the only means available for

conversation starters and repairs. By fully focusing all thoughts on one topic, he can reduce the degree of anxiety inherent in unknown situations. Unfortunately, this very technique to create harmony within his environment also severely limits his thinking skills. He cannot spontaneously perceive information outside his narrow, restricted range without complaint. Such behavior severely limits his play skills with peers to the point where arguments develop or he is ultimately shunned as being too "weird."

Direct attempts designed to reduce this rigidity in the child often just increase his anxiety and frustration. He will no longer be able to follow his self-imposed scripts and, therefore, his ability to control the conversation. The comforting sense of conversational control he so eagerly craves is no longer available to him. He is now forced to participate in the outside world, which has rules he cannot interpret; his lack of flexibility becomes more apparent. As his anxiety increases, he attempts to return the conversation to his control. Lacking an adequate command of conversational repairs, he is limited to direct statements that his listeners often consider verbally abusive. Recognizing that his attempt to redirect the conversation back to his comfort zone has failed, he is now bound to use the only method left available to him. His frustration has rapidly expanded and he is now filled with rage. He explodes in a rage-induced meltdown.

When an individual is limited in the number of approaches available to him to produce a desired change, he often resorts to the most drastic means. Explosive rage, while not socially acceptable, frequently achieves the desired result. The classic "terrible twos" used to describe the behaviors of two-year-olds is a prime example. Two-year-olds, though, get into trouble by wandering and exploring as they attempt to learn more about their environment. The behaviors of the three-year-old child are more analogous to Asperger's Syndrome than the "terrible twos." Limited in their available vocabulary to express their demands and/or emotional states, three-year-olds frequently resort to shouting, "No!" When this fails to produce the desired result, they have temper tantrums. These temper tantrums serve a functional purpose and communicate a specific message. The wise parent does not allow this behavior to become fixated but rather attempts to provide the child with more socially appropriate means to express his displeasure. Wiser yet is the parent who recognizes that preventing these episodes from developing is easier to accomplish than trying to defuse a rage episode once it erupts.

Such is the case with Asperger's Syndrome. The old adage *An ounce of prevention is worth a pound of cure* should be the mantra for those working with children with Asperger's Syndrome. It is ultimately easier to manage children through adaptive supports and the elimination of as many negative triggers as possible.

This constant difficulty with social skills does not go unnoticed by children with Asperger's Syndrome. In their early years, they may not be astute enough to recognize their differences. However, as they enter their teens, the differences become more apparent. These adolescents desire friendships, just as any other child does, but they are at a loss as to how to acquire friends and keep them. For these individuals, the constant sense of rejection may become overwhelming, leading to reduced self-esteem and possibly depression. Their inability to verbalize their inner emotional feelings creates further difficulty, and a downward spiral may begin to develop. Teachers should be aware of this trait and not rely on verbal responses from these children to ascertain their emotional status. All those associated with children with Asperger's Syndrome must constantly be alert and vigilant for signs of depression, especially for adolescents with Asperger's Syndrome. Since verbal responses will not be an adequate source of information, adults must rely on changes in behavior for signals of depression. Changes in dress, mood, loneliness, and fatigue may all be symptomatic of clinical depression. Should these traits be evidenced, referral for appropriate psychiatric management is strongly recommended.

➤ Social/Emotional Checklist

The Social/Emotional Checklist, pages 78-79, is provided to allow you an opportunity to quickly reflect on the various behaviors that *may* be seen in a student diagnosed with Asperger's Syndrome. Compare the student's current behavior with respect to these questions and relate them to the various diagnostic criteria discussed in Chapter 1 (e.g., *DSM-IV TR*, *ICD-10*, and Gillberg's Criteria).

Social/Emotional Checklist

Student: _____   Date: _____

School: _____   Evaluator: _____

Check each item that applies to the student in comparison with same-aged peers. The presence of these characteristics or behaviors may suggest the presence of Asperger's Syndrome and/or facilitate selecting appropriate intervention goals. Elaborate with examples or additional comments as warranted.

➢ Social-Interactive

☐ Does the child lack tact?

☐ Does the child have poor proxemics?

☐ Does the child appear to have difficulty with social rules?

☐ Does the child appear to be egocentric?

☐ Does the child fail to understand jokes?

☐ Does the child appear to be overly naive?

☐ Does the child have obsessive interests?

☐ Does the child have trouble relating outside his area of interest?

☐ Does the child have poor play skills?

☐ Does the child appear to dislike physical contact?

☐ Is the child easily taken advantage of?

➤ Social-Communicative

- ☐ Does the child display pedantic speech?

- ☐ Does the child have difficulty initiating and terminating conversation?

- ☐ Does the child have prosodic speech deficits?

- ☐ Does the child perseverate on questions?

- ☐ Does the child appear to have deficits in abstract reasoning?

- ☐ Does the child demonstrate poor nonverbal communication skills?

➤ Social-Emotional

- ☐ Does the child appear to be easily stressed?

- ☐ Does the child have low self-esteem?

- ☐ Does the child appear to exhibit signs and symptoms of depression?

- ☐ Does change overwhelm the child?

- ☐ Does the child seem overly anxious?

- ☐ Does the child engage in rituals?

- ☐ Does the child experience sensory overload?

> Treatment Strategies

Direct Instruction for Social Skills

Social skills come naturally for most people. We make social mistakes and are capable of realizing them. Based on our analysis of situations, we make accommodations, thereby becoming more proficient in our social skills. Individuals with Asperger's Syndrome appear to lack this innate capacity to develop social skills. Although everyone else acquires social skills through osmosis, the individual with Asperger's Syndrome must instead rely on direct instruction.

Most individuals with Asperger's Syndrome fail to recognize that their actions have a direct effect on others. It is difficult to change a behavior when the behavior to change is not perceived as inadequate or counterproductive. It is imperative, then, that instruction in social skills incorporate not only instruction directed to the individual but also to those who associate with him.

Perhaps the easiest way to accomplish this training is through peer and adult education. It is human nature to avoid what is different or unusual. Once the unfamiliar becomes familiar, though, our trepidation decreases, allowing for greater interaction. Providing educational opportunities to those who associate with the individual with Asperger's Syndrome makes the person's peculiar behaviors less astonishing. As a result, the atypical behaviors the individual exhibits produce less attention, thereby allowing for greater acceptance and decreasing the likelihood of teasing or misinterpretation.

Alternative Instruction

Despite the good intentions behind direct instruction for these students, some parents may not approve of having their children singled out from their classmates. In these instances, the concerns of the parents must be respected. Instead of relating how one particular child's behavior is unique, it may be more appropriate to incorporate a generalized disability awareness program. Doing so eliminates the necessity for legal releases and parental approval. Such programs may include a wide variety of topics, such as blindness, deafness, and physical disabilities. The astute instructor will simply include a greater number of examples specific to the unique traits of Asperger's Syndrome, thereby accomplishing the same result without calling attention to the individual.

Buddy systems are another means of enabling greater acceptance. Teachers have long used a buddy system to assure homework assignments have been properly written down in assignment books. The peer buddy system can be expanded to coaching in given areas such as reading, writing, and play activities. By nature, children generally like to stand out from the crowd. Assigning different children the responsibility of being a peer buddy throughout the day affords many students an opportunity to shine, and it becomes even more inviting when those who volunteer are perceived as belonging to the "in" crowd. Take care, though, not to repeatedly delegate this responsibility to the same child. Strive to generate a sense of entitled privilege rather than a sense of drudgery.

Nonverbal Language

Individuals with Asperger's Syndrome invariably fail to recognize the impact their behavior has on those around them. In addition, they also do not know how to modify their behavior according to the needs of a given situation. These students need specific instruction that promotes self-realization and greater self-monitoring of their behavior.

Recognizing and responding to the nonverbal signals a listener provides is a crucial area for instruction. Facial features, eye gaze, gestures, and body postures all communicate messages. Most individuals not challenged by the deficits associated with Asperger's Syndrome have no difficulty reading the nonverbal manner in which emotions are "spoken," be they negative (e.g., boredom, anger, frustration) or positive (e.g., excitement, desire, interest). Photographs and videotapes have been found to aid in the recognition of various emotions and have successfully been used to produce a desired change. Enhancing the ability to recognize nonverbal messages in others gives individuals with Asperger's Syndrome greater skill and confidence in monitoring their social interactions.

Changing Social Behavior

Several techniques have been used successfully to teach better socialization. Social stories (Gray, 1995) are an effective way to teach appropriate social interactions. Their strength lies in their simplistic ability to remain flexible and responsive to a variety of needs. They may incorporate text and/or pictures to describe situations from an individual's perspective and offer suitable choices for the desired outcome. The usefulness of this technique cannot be exaggerated as it remains an indispensable tool for effectuating change in social behavior.

Individualized, Immediate Feedback

Another technique designed by Carol Gray is comic-strip conversations (Gray, 1994). Similar to social stories, comic-strip conversations incorporate simplistic drawings of individuals in classic comic-strip fashion. Through the use of verbal bubbles and various visual cues, the individual with Asperger's Syndrome can analyze the nature of a conversation in greater detail. These simple drawings can direct attention to how individuals initiate, maintain, and/or terminate a conversation.

Lavoie's social autopsy technique provides useful feedback to help students understand how a specific social interaction failed to produce the desired effect (Bieber, 1994). Allowing the individual who committed a social blunder to immediately meet with an appropriate adult in a private setting, identifies the error and reviews steps to take to avoid repeating the error in the future. For individuals with Asperger's Syndrome, it may be necessary to adapt this technique by incorporating visual supports to assure appropriate comprehension. It is not meant to be a form of punishment, nor should it be viewed as a negative consequence. Rather, it is a course of action designed to help the individual recognize and analyze his error in an attempt to produce a positive change.

Abstract Language

In many instances, difficulties in social interaction are directly related to a deficiency in the recognition and use of abstract language. Many individuals with Asperger's Syndrome require direct instruction in recognizing and comprehending idioms, metaphors, and words with multiple meanings. Implied meanings and inferences are further areas of difficulty requiring direct instruction.

Individualized Instruction

Individual skills designed to increase appropriate interpersonal interaction are essential. Depending on the needs of the student, it may be necessary to teach how to wait in line. For an individual with Asperger's Syndrome, the importance of something as basic as waiting in line may be a foreign concept. Young children may require visual supports to assist them in learning this skill. Footprints, color coding, and reference lines all can help children develop better control in this area.

Structured Play Groups

Structured play groups allow children with Asperger's Syndrome to practice specific techniques under the guidance of trained individuals. Through this technique, children are provided opportunities to practice and engage in activities in areas free of distraction. By providing specific items known to be of interest to the child, the instructor can facilitate the child's attention to his use of the toys and objects as well as his face. Later, as the child becomes more capable of participating in these tangential play activities, introduce tasks allowing for greater social interaction and requiring the student to request assistance.

For structured play activities to succeed, the instructor must recognize the need to imitate the child's actions in a manner that draws attention to his actions and not to the toys themselves. He should position himself in such a way that the child's gaze can easily perceive his expressions. By matching the child's actions, exaggerating the responses, and providing slight variation to avoid establishing a routine, the instructor can produce positive changes in the child's socialization and interactions. Introducing more complex toys and objects, as well as different people and settings, can expand these activities to allow for new opportunities for interaction to be developed, facilitating more complex language structures and social interactions.

Taking Others' Perspectives

All individuals with Asperger's Syndrome have difficulty in taking someone else's perspective. These individuals often do not recognize that others have feelings and attitudes different from their own. Such an egocentric view of the world does not allow for appropriate social interaction. Instruction designed to enhance the development of perspective taking should be a critical component in any treatment program for Asperger's Syndrome.

Simple activities in which the various likes and dislikes of classmates are listed for direct comparison and discussion allow children with Asperger's Syndrome an opportunity to learn of others' interests. Barrier games are another interesting activity to assist in perspective taking. They allow participants to quickly realize that what someone said is frequently not what the person meant. Incorporating barrier games into perspective-taking activities helps students to understand things from someone else's perspective.

Drama is another way to teach students to take someone else's perspective and to interact appropriately in social situations. Simple activities may afford opportunities for practicing a variety of emotions and appropriate reactions to them. As the child practices a drama, you can teach her how the relationship between specific actions, or lack of actions, impacts social interchange. Imitating others' responses allows the child with Asperger's Syndrome an opportunity to see firsthand how these skills can be employed. It may be necessary to have other students model various styles of social interaction before expecting the child with Asperger's Syndrome to attempt to perform these herself. These drama activities may focus on specific social actions and provide the child with Asperger's Syndrome an advantage not afforded in other settings. By structuring these activities around specific social interactions, instructors can reinforce those areas where the child is having success as well as provide opportunities for learning new skills in a highly structured environment.

Focusing Attention

A child with Asperger's Syndrome may focus on completely irrelevant, unrelated items within pictures, so it is necessary to make sure the child's attention is being directed to the intended topic and not to some irrelevant item. For the teacher, it is extremely frustrating to find that your student hasn't the vaguest idea of what you have been talking about, even though it appeared he was attending. The wise teacher knows that her agenda is generally not the same as her students', yet general education students can be easily redirected to the appropriate task. Children with Asperger's Syndrome, however, are oftentimes completely uninterested in the regular education agenda and resist attempts by others to change their attention focus.

Small-Group Activities

Small-group activities are frequently employed in the general education curriculum. They afford wonderful opportunities for cooperative learning. Unfortunately, they create situations that are troublesome for children with Asperger's Syndrome. By their nature, these group activities require the students to interact positively so that learning occurs. This teaching technique may be appropriate for many students, but unless the child with Asperger's Syndrome has been instructed how to participate in such a group, it is a recipe for disaster. The child may attempt to lead the group and resist anyone's efforts at offering suggestions. Failing to recognize that cooperative learning requires participation by all students, the child may incorrectly judge peer suggestions as personal attacks and not as options to be explored. To avoid situations like these, instruct children with Asperger's Syndrome how to participate in small-group activities. These students require instruction in recognizing that other individuals may have different views from their own and, more importantly, how to accept these views.

To achieve this skill, clearly delineate each individual's role and responsibility within the group, especially the role of the student with Asperger's Syndrome. Do not assume that this student is capable of rapidly generalizing one skill to multiple situations. It may be necessary to point out the similarities visually to ensure that carryover will occur.

In addition, students with Asperger's Syndrome may require direct instruction about sharing. Many schools require groups of students to share equipment due to funding issues, especially in science labs with microscopes, specimens, and other necessary high-cost equipment. Unless students with Asperger's Syndrome have received specific techniques and strategies designed to assist them in learning how to share, these children will rapidly encounter problems in sharing such equipment.

These students view the world as black and white. Classmates are either with them or against them. Do not allow these individuals to persist in their egocentric perception of the world. Give them opportunities to realize that the best choice is often obtained from brainstorming sessions that explore a variety of options. Do not allow these students to become verbally abusive. Their lack of social understanding will create situations in which they cannot compromise or debate. These individuals must be taught empathy and appropriate social techniques to solve arguments. Recognizing, predicting, and responding appropriately to another person's viewpoint require specific teaching.

Direct instruction in how to respond to both praise and criticism should also be provided. Teaching the strategy of observing others to see how they react in similar situations may further refine these skills. Learning to cooperate and compromise does not come naturally for students with Asperger's Syndrome. They depend on others for formal instruction.

Cooperation and Compromise

Cooperation requires mutual understanding. It requires perspective taking and flexibility. These are areas in which individuals with

Asperger's Syndrome have extreme difficulty. Unless they are provided with opportunities to enhance this flexibility of thought, their abilities to cooperate and compromise will suffer. Set-shifting games are one technique found to promote greater flexibility in thought. These games require individuals to rapidly regroup a series of words or objects into various sets. Doing so allows them to recognize that many possibilities are available to them and that there is no single, correct answer. For example, present students with various shapes cut from colored card stock in a variety of sizes. Ask the students to organize the objects according to shape, then size, then color, etc. By rapidly changing the task, the children realize that multiple options are available for grouping the objects.

Figure-ground reversal illusions are another opportunity for these children to practice flexibility of thought. These tasks require looking at a picture to discover imbedded information. Words or pictures may be used to enhance the individual's flexibility. Common examples of these tasks are pictures in which a series of pictures are hidden. The fun is in attempting to locate all the hidden pictures in the shortest amount of time possible. Another example is a picture that, when viewed in just the correct manner, produces an embedded, three-dimensional picture.

Stroop-like tasks (Stroop, 1935) also enhance flexible thinking. These tasks involve presenting information in a novel means and requiring students to identify the items according to a set pattern. For example, multiple copies of the words *big* and *little* are printed on a piece of paper. Some words are written in lowercase letters and others in uppercase. The manner in which the words are presented is entirely random. Instead of reading the series of words aloud, the individual is required to rapidly state the size of the case used for either the word *big* or *little*. For example, if you were presented with the following: *LITTLE – little – big – LITTLE – BIG – big* and told to identify the case of the word *little*, your response would be "big, little, big" because the case of the word *little* is first in uppercase ("big"), then lowercase ("little"), and then in uppercase.

You can change this task to identifying the word based on a specific case, such as "Read only the little (lowercase) words." Then the answer would be "little, big, big."

Another type of Stroop task involves presenting color words (*red*, *green*, *blue*, etc.) printed in different colors. The choice of color a word is written in is purely random. However, a color cannot be used if the name of it is not included in the list. For example, if a random presentation of the following words is used — *red, green, black, blue, yellow, orange* — the colors these words are printed in must incorporate the same color palate. Thus the word *red* is printed using red, green, black, yellow, blue, and orange ink. The same color ink is used for all the other words. No pattern should be used in the presentation of the words and the words do not have to be presented equally. The task involves set shifting from "Name all the words printed in green ink" (an easy task) to "Tell me the color ink used only for the word *green* throughout the entire page" (a much more difficult task). Flexibility of thought can be improved by incorporating these techniques into daily activities, and with that improvement, an improvement in social flexibility will also occur.

Capitalizing on Strengths

Teachers should find students' strengths and capitalize on them for the good of all. Children with Asperger's Syndrome often shine when their idiosyncratic learning relates to the current school agenda. For example, some of these students may excel at spelling. As a result, these children may be highly desirable members of a spelling bee team. Likewise, children who are math wizards may be sought after for peer tutoring.

Conversation Training

Since conversation is extremely difficult for individuals with Asperger's Syndrome, structured tasks designed to increase fundamental conversation skills is necessary. Skills such as how to initiate a conversation, how to take turns, and how to expand the conversation are all appropriate goals. These skills can be taught using the four parameters of Grice's Maxims (Grice, 1975). Teaching the concepts of *Quantity, Quality, Relation*, and *Manner* can improve conversational skills. The simplicity behind Grice's Maxims is the driving force for its success.

Quantity, the first maxim, means saying just enough and not too much — a concern for individuals with Asperger's Syndrome. It involves determining whether a conversation carried the proper amount of information to allow it to develop. Controlling the quantity of conversation limits the tendency for an individual to dominate the conversation and reduces the chances of lecturing. If a conversation is to develop well, the speaker must limit the amount of time devoted to a specific topic.

Grice's second maxim, *Quality*, deals with the truthfulness of the speaker's information. In many cases, individuals with Asperger's Syndrome tend to superimpose their own views and opinions as though they are factual information. This is especially important in situations in which the speaker must summarize factual information.

The third maxim, *Relation*, requires the speaker to determine the relevancy of the information presented. This skill is extremely important for individuals with Asperger's Syndrome to learn. They frequently superimpose their obsessive interests on a conversation without regard to the relevancy to the actual topic at hand. These individuals can be taught to review their input to improve the relevancy of their comments in a conversation.

The last maxim, *Manner*, relates to the clarity of the speaker's information. Analyzing the clarity of a conversation improves verbal precision. Too often, individuals with Asperger's Syndrome have a tendency toward verbal mazing, confusing their listeners. Controlling for clarity improves the precision of conversation.

All four of the principals behind Grice's Maxims relate directly to conversational issues inherent in individuals with Asperger's Syndrome.

Instruction in active listening skills is also appropriate, thereby allowing for a reduction in interruptions and allowing for greater conversational expansion to occur. The practical techniques outlined by Nan Stutzman Eller (Eller, 1992) are designed to increase active listening skills. She approaches active listening by teaching how to recognize and improve listening attitudes and by teaching people to be accountable for their own listening. Incorporating these techniques during conversations yields gains in auditory attention, memory, and comprehension. In addition to these techniques, it may be necessary to teach how to recognize and use contextual cues to increase comprehension of both auditory and written information. Until students with Asperger's Syndrome have increased their competence with comprehension, it may be wise to use simpler language when speaking with them, especially when providing instructions.

Not knowing what to say or do when communication problems arise is a frequent difficulty. The simple request to repeat something may seem obvious to many, but those with Asperger's Syndrome may require direct instruction in this skill. Hence, consider teaching specific strategies designed to repair conversational breakdowns. It is important to know what to say when you are confused and how to politely correct your listener when you have been misunderstood. Such skills allow a speaker to revise or repair mistakes to avoid potential problems. Role-playing, social stories, social autopsies, and comic-strip conversations are all excellent means of teaching these skills.

Eye Contact

Some individuals with Asperger's Syndrome have a tendency for poor eye contact. Nothing implies a lack of interest better than failing to provide adequate eye contact during a conversation. Formal instruction designed to increase eye contact should be avoided because it has a tendency to produce staring, a trait that is just as irritating as having no eye contact. Rather, encourage appropriate eye contact through a variety of indirect means.

Shared visual experiences are an excellent means of improving appropriate eye contact. Appropriate eye gaze may be reinforced through joint attention to visual stimuli. Looking at artwork, photography, etc., allows both the student and teacher's attention to be directed toward the intended object and then back to one another. This kind of eye engagement may be repeated several times, allowing for variety in the time spent looking at the objects and one another. In this manner, the student does not sense the degree of anxiety associated with the direct eye gaze commonly used in conversation. Guiding the child's eyes through subtle hand movements may also produce the desired result. At times, a simple, but honest, discussion in the style of a social story may improve eye contact.

Quite frequently, individuals with Asperger's Syndrome don't understand the rationale for using eye contact. The need to "connect" with a conversational partner through eye contact remains a foreign concept for these individuals. The goal, therefore, is not to produce direct eye contact but to increase the understanding of why and how people use eye contact.

Self-Confidence

Individuals with Asperger's Syndrome know something is different about them. They are teased incessantly simply because they don't fit in. Unlike their peers, children with Asperger's Syndrome have not learned strategies to deal with teasing. They cannot recognize sarcasm and cannot retort with some witty comeback of their own. Rather than provide direct instruction in this area, it may be more advisable for the adult staff to remain vigilant to these concerns to protect these children from teasing. Without adult intervention, teasing may contribute to a poor self-image and, ultimately, depression. Not being able to adequately put feelings into words may eventually lead to feelings of doubt and poor self-confidence. Strategies designed to enhance self-confidence and self-image are highly recommended. Without such strategies, these children will inevitably withdraw and become reclusive. Those who deal with these children should be aware of this potential consequence and deal with it accordingly.

Too often these children are allowed to retreat into their own little worlds, with little intervention provided to redirect their attention to more socially acceptable interactions. Since these children do not actively express their emotional status effectively, they will continue to retreat to safe havens. Their comfort associated with consistency far outweighs their desire to establish more socially appropriate interactions. Treatment designed to increase their flexibility, both cognitively and socially, will assist in reducing their compulsion to maintain consistency and uniformity.

Predictability

The demand for uniformity among individuals with Asperger's Syndrome permeates almost all activities of daily living. This need for consistency and uniformity allows an opportunity to capitalize on it to produce desired social change. Since changes in day-to-day activities cause excessive anxiety, creating an environment that affords a sense of predictability will decrease the degree of anxiety associated with change and allow for greater self-control.

Classrooms should be designed with this concept in mind. For younger children, centers of activity afford a sense of assurance. It is comforting to know that reading can be associated with the beanbag chairs and art activities at the art table. Rooms that rely on changing the overall structure based on the task at hand do not afford children the ability to predict what is upcoming.

Classroom Group Interaction

Many teachers employ social understanding when introducing new or novel information. Groups of children may be assigned to specific work clusters within the classroom for collaborative sharing of information. It is not uncommon for teachers to have students research specific topics as a group. Social studies classes often use collaborative sharing of information. Groups of students may be assigned individual topics, such as a given state or country, and required to present their findings to the class. In some classes, students may be required to share equipment or listen as a group to a set of instructions. Science classes are a prime example of collaborative sharing. They frequently demand students to pair up or work in small groups with specialized equipment. The high cost associated with equipment, such as microscopes, consumables, and prepared specimens for dissection, frequently necessitates the need for small-group settings.

It may be wiser if the child with Asperger's Syndrome is afforded the opportunity to work independently. While this strategy may seem exclusionary, the child with Asperger's Syndrome may appreciate the opportunity to progress at his own speed without the added stress of social interaction inherent in such small-group settings. However, to assist the child in learning appropriate interactions in small-group settings, it may be necessary to provide him with direct instruction in the various roles each member of the group plays and the responsibilities associated with each role. The child with Asperger's Syndrome may perceive interplay among the students in a group as threatening. She may perceive suggestions associated with group brainstorming as personal attacks and demonstrate inappropriate reactions and responses. Children with Asperger's Syndrome need to learn negotiation skills to provide them with better interpersonal skills in academic groupings.

Environmental Organization

Concepts of environmental organization as employed in the Treatment and Education of Autistic and Communication Handicapped Children (TEACCH) model (Schopler et al., 1995) may also afford greater comfort to the child with Asperger's Syndrome. Developed in North Carolina, the TEACCH concept relies on adapting the environment as much as possible to accommodate the unique learning styles inherent within the autism spectrum. Clear visual boundaries are provided to segment space into recognizable areas. Such boundaries provide the children an opportunity to understand what is expected within each area. The degree of distraction, both visual and auditory, is modified based on the demands associated with each activity. The result is an environment that allows for increased production with a minimum of distress.

"Safety"

No matter how proactive a teacher may try to be, there will inevitably be instances where the child with Asperger's Syndrome will experience circumstances she deems stressful. Identifying locations that the child determines as "safe" offers a sense of security. An example of such a safe space may be a specific desk within the classroom as free of clutter and distraction as possible. The guidance office, assistant principal's office, or library may all afford a sense of tranquility for the child with Asperger's Syndrome. In addition to providing a safe location, it may be wise to provide the student a specific person deemed as her "safe" person. This individual may offer limited guidance and provide for opportunities to employ various relaxation techniques.

Too often, good intentions are hampered by the assumption that all children will find comfort in the same location. Just as each child presents with unique idiosyncrasies, each safe place should be specifically selected for each child. It is necessary to assess the needs of each child individually and not presume consistency among all. A predictable, safe environment is of utmost concern when managing children with Asperger's Syndrome.

Transitions

Transitions also tend to create stress for children with Asperger's Syndrome. It is wise to minimize the degree of transitions afforded to these children. A self-contained classroom may be more suitable for them than changing rooms each period. Likewise, transitions from task-to-task within the classroom may create difficulty.

It may help to use visual supports designed specifically for transitions. Visual supports have been shown to ease transitions for many individuals. Unlike auditory information, in which the message is transitory, visual information is constant. It affords greater processing time and reduces the demands created by social interaction.

Scheduling Tools

Schedules are an indispensable tool. Everyone uses schedules on a daily basis. In school, we use them to assist in learning our class schedule. In the work setting, we use personal information management tools, either computer based, such as a *Palm*™ *Pilot*, or print based, such as a *Day-Timer*®. These tools allow us to effortlessly plan for upcoming events and assist us in remembering when we have scheduled them.

Similar schedules can be afforded to the child with Asperger's Syndrome. We can use daily, weekly, and monthly calendars to denote changes in the child's routine. Calendars may also be used to indicate new or novel events, such as an upcoming field trip or holiday. Calendars are indispensable for alerting the child to major schedule changes associated with block schedules or semester-based classes. Simple reminders, such as highlighting the day of a field trip, allow the child an opportunity to adequately prepare for the change or transitions involved.

In addition to visually alerting the child to upcoming events, these schedules and calendars help the child develop a richer concept of time. Use care when developing schedules and checklists as some individuals may reject them on the grounds of being "different." When making schedules, try to be as discrete as possible, taking into consideration the size of the schedule and needs of the child to remain within the mainstream. Bookmark-sized schedules have been found to be readily accepted in part because of their small size and ease of use.

In addition to formal calendars and schedules, simple contingency statements such as "First–Then" prompts are also effective in reducing the problems attributed to transitions. Following is an example of this type of contingency statement:

(See page 96 for a blank "First-Then" page that can be reproduced and used with students as needed.)

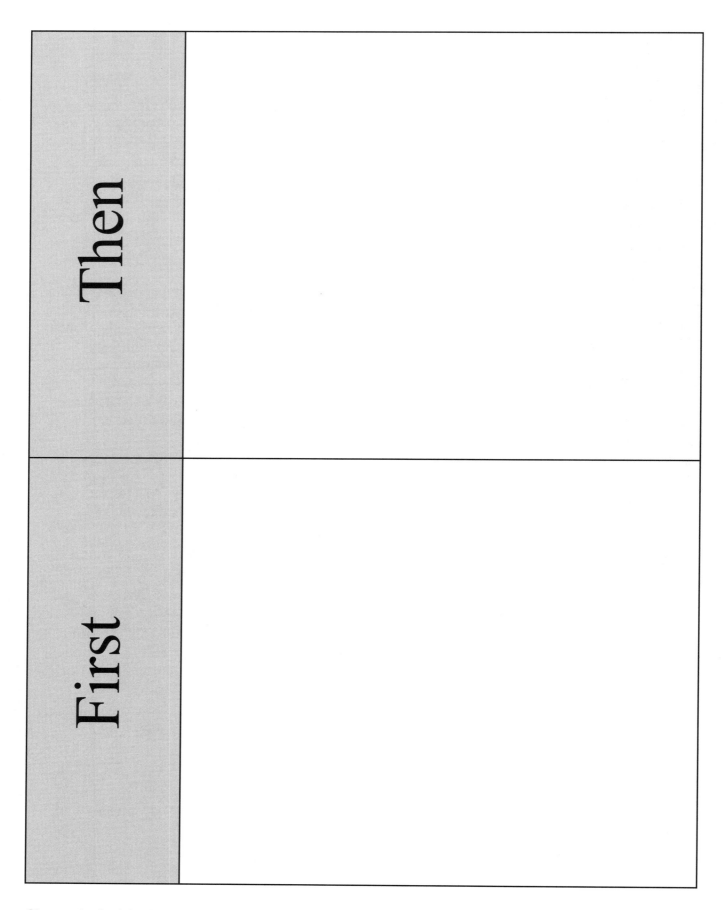

Checklists

Checklists are effective tools for many individuals. Few of us can complete our grocery shopping without them. Likewise, children with Asperger's Syndrome can be taught to use checklists appropriately. Many schools have instituted daily planners to help children remember what items need to be brought home. These planners may be further refined for use in a specific class or subject. Their use provides the clear, concise information children need to increase appropriate transitions. By allowing students the opportunity to recognize beforehand what needs to be accomplished, we help them readily anticipate the need for change and thereby transition between tasks more easily.

Daily Routines

For many people, *luxury* means sleeping late and having a leisurely brunch while catching up on some overdue reading. To the child with Asperger's Syndrome, however, not knowing when to get up, what to have for breakfast, what to wear, when to get dressed, etc., is a recipe for disaster. Daily routines assist many children with Asperger's Syndrome to organize their day in a consistent manner. Choosing the next day's attire before going to bed eliminates that potentially anxiety-producing activity in the morning. Having a consistent routine for the morning ritual of bathing, dressing, and eating creates a sense of security and, more importantly, fewer problems for parents. This is one area where checklists are essential. Capitalize on the child's need for consistency to avoid surprises, thereby diminishing the turmoil and anxiety associated with the unknown.

Surprises and the Unknown

A surefire method of creating uncertainty is to yell, "Surprise!" The anxiety meter will inevitably soar, leading to unexpected results. For many children, surprises are exciting events worthy of intense conversation. However, for children with Asperger's Syndrome, surprises create untold anxiety. Their daily routine is no longer consistent. What lies ahead cannot be predicted, and with this loss, the ability to self-modulate behavior becomes nearly impossible. Pop quizzes, new seating arrangements, substitute teachers, etc., are disasters waiting to happen. Surprises, therefore, are best avoided at all cost.

Unfortunately, children with Asperger's Syndrome constantly fear the unknown. Unable to predict the world around them or to make sense out of the indiscernible cues required in social settings, these children experience undue stress. To help children interpret these ever-changing situations, it is paramount to calm their fears regarding the unknown. Providing them an avenue to make sense out of their environment offers children with Asperger's Syndrome a chance to establish some degree of tranquility. Maps, cue cards, and practice sessions all reduce the anxiety of new tasks. To help a middle school or high school student learn the layout of a new school or schedule, employ a "dry-run" to allow the student an opportunity to rehearse the pattern when no other classmates are present. Be proactive by recognizing that the newness associated with unfamiliar settings and people will increase anxiety. Provide opportunities to introduce the individual to these situations and people in less stressful settings. Stay alert to identify those areas in which the child's fear of the unknown is negatively impacting his daily performance; be ready to offer assistance.

Expanding Interest Range

In their attempt to reduce the degree of anxiety associated with unfamiliar situations, individuals with Asperger's Syndrome often limit their interest range to extremely narrow topics, many of which are not typically found in the general population. These children may resist all attempts at engaging them outside their narrow interest ranges and call further attention to their difficulties in social interaction and communication.

What does one do with a child who has extremely limited interests and insists on rigidly adhering to such interests no matter what? This formidable task may be adapted through relatively uncomplicated means. Many people find that the amount of time the child spends dwelling on a topic is more irritating than the topic itself.

Knowing that Thomas will most likely want to talk about telephone poles allows us an opportunity to prepare ourselves. We simply accept the fact that Thomas will want to talk about them. We see him and immediately think "telephone poles." If he would limit the amount of time spent on telephone poles, our ability to tolerate him would increase.

The challenge, then, is to provide the individual with techniques that will successfully limit the amount of time spent on his obsessive interest. Auditory prompts do not work. Thomas will continue talking about telephone poles, despite being told numerous times to discontinue the topic. It is as if his auditory loop is ineffective. The key is to use visual supports. Two supports highly effective in reducing the amount of time spent talking about a particular topic are traffic signals and a Time Timer™ (Generaction, Inc., 7707 Camargo Road, Cincinnati, OH 45243, 877-771-8463).

Pictures of traffic signals can also be used to limit the amount of time spent talking on a topic. Draw a simple picture of a classic traffic signal on one side of an index card. Color the top circle red. On the reverse side of the card, draw another traffic signal. Color the bottom circle green.

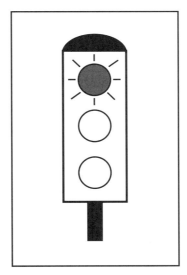 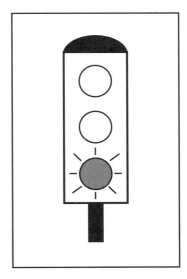

When the green side is shown, the child may "go" on talking. However, when the red side is shown, the child must "stop" talking. The appropriate side is shown to the child to provide a visual cue, thereby allowing him to monitor his conversation more effectively. Any individual may use this visual means of support. For some individuals,

the written word may be just as effective. However, visual representations using pictographs are generally much more effective than the written word as exemplified by the fact that many individuals find analog clocks much faster to process than digital clocks. The size of the visual support is not as important as the consistency with which it is applied. A haphazard approach will not yield the desired result and will quickly be abandoned as useless.

The Time Timer™ has also been shown to produce a marked decrease in the amount of time spent perseverating on a given topic. It displays a section of bright red to denote a specific time period, similar to the timers attached to bombs in James Bond movies. As the period of time decreases, the amount of red showing slowly decreases until eventually none is left. The Time Timer™ differs from digital timers in that it eliminates the problems associated with fixating on the numbers and reactions to audible alarms.

No matter which visual support you use, provide explanations to the child that will incorporate him into the therapeutic process. Allowing him an opportunity to recognize the reason behind the request to cease talking increases the chances that he will actively use this strategy effectively. Immediate, positive reinforcement will serve to further increase his ability to self-monitor his conversation.

Another technique to broaden children's range of interests is to capitalize on their current interest levels. If academic tasks can be modified such that they superficially appear to relate to children's interest areas, children with Asperger's Syndrome can be enticed into performing a wide variety of academic activities. Thomas, our telephone pole expert, has absolutely no interest in math word problems and may refuse to participate in any activity in which they are present. However, math word problems can easily be adapted around Thomas's obsessive interest in telephone poles. For example, incorporating telephone poles into the task can modify the famous word problem in which a train leaves New York while an identical train simultaneously leaves Los Angeles. The modified question now reads *A train leaves New York carrying wood soon to be made into telephone poles, while an identical train leaves Los Angeles carrying creosote used in preserving telephone poles . . . .* Even though the computational design of the math problem did not change, Thomas may be more interested in working on solving this problem because now it incorporates telephone poles. The effort required to motivate

Thomas to participate was minimal. Chances are, had the teacher insisted that he complete the task without incorporating telephone poles, a power struggle would have developed.

Interest levels can be expanded by slowly incorporating changes into the adapted word problem. For example, the teacher may use the adapted problem as written above, but adapt it further by indicating that sudden engine problems with the train carrying creosote necessitated a last-minute substitution with one that was carrying automobiles. Thomas may still complete the task because his obsessive interest remains in the word problem. By slowly including other items and gradually decreasing the frequency with which telephone poles are used, the teacher may persuade Thomas to participate in class activities. By incorporating these strategies, it is possible to use the rigidity associated with obsessional interests as a means of enticing compliance. This approach will ultimately expand the child's extremely limited interest area.

The following Suggestions for Intervention, pages 102-105, summarize the techniques reviewed in this chapter. They are provided for your convenience in considering appropriate intervention with individual students with Asperger's Syndrome.

➢ Suggestions for Intervention

Social-Interactive

➢ Teach the relationship the child's actions or inactions have on others in the environment. Teach how to modify behavior accordingly.

➢ Incorporate not only the child in social skills training but also those around him.

➢ Incorporate peer education through disability awareness programs.

➢ Use buddy systems.

➢ Use structured play groups and vary the children within the groups.

➢ Use social stories.

➢ Use comic-strip conversations.

➢ Use social autopsies.

➢ Teach how to wait in line.

➢ Teach perspective taking.

➢ Teach sharing skills.

➢ Teach negotiation skills.

➢ Teach responsibilities and roles for given situations.

➢ Teach how to work in small groups.

➢ Help the student gain respect through academic strengths.

➢ Protect the individual from teasing.

➢ Do not allow the student to become reclusive.

➢ Teach social interaction through drama activities.

➢ Use visual organization tools, such as schedules, calendars, and checklists.

➢ Establish routines.

➤ Teach flexibility of thought.

➤ Use set-shifting games.

➤ Use figure-ground reversal illusions.

➤ Use Stroop-like tasks.

➤ Teach methods to assist in transitions.

➤ Use contingency statements.

➤ Teach how to imitate others.

➤ Teach how to accept others' views.

➤ Teach how to solve an argument.

➤ Teach how to deal with teasing.

➤ Teach the student to model his behavior after a student who behaves appropriately.

Social-Communicative

➤ Ensure attention is being directed to the intended topic and not to some irrelevant item.

➤ Teach conversational skills.

➤ Teach active listening.

➤ Teach conversational repair strategies.

➤ Do not formally teach eye contact; encourage it via natural activities.

➤ Limit the amount of time the child devotes to a specific topic.

➤ Teach mutual focus.

➤ Teach Grice's Maxims.

➤ Teach techniques to adapt conversational topic and style to the listener's needs.

➤ Use barrier games.

➤ Teach prosodic variation.

> Teach recognizing and responding to nonverbal signals.

> Teach abstract language.

> Teach idioms.

> Teach metaphors.

> Teach implied meanings.

> Teach multiple-meaning words.

> Teach contextual cues.

> Use simple language for instructions.

> Teach how to respond to praise.

> Teach how to respond to criticism.

> Teach gestures.

> Teach recognition and use of facial features.

> Teach the student to model his behavior after a student who behaves appropriately.

Social-Emotional

> Recognize signs of depression and refer for appropriate management.

> Increase self-esteem.

> Do not formally teach eye contact, encourage it.

> Develop nonverbal techniques for appropriate feedback.

> Formally teach how to recognize various emotions in self and others.

> Teach how to express emotions verbally and nonverbally.

> Provide a safe haven.

> Use positive or unemotional tone of voice when engaging the child.

> Provide a safe person during times of emotional stress.

➚ Teach what to say or do when problems arise.

➚ Teach the student to observe others to see how they react.

➚ Teach relaxation techniques.

➚ Decrease anxiety regarding the unknown via prior introduction.

➚ Use positive reinforcement.

➚ Teach empathy.

➚ Teach the student to predict another person's viewpoint.

Chapter 7:
Academic Issues

 ## Skills & Deficits

Attending

Perhaps Individuals with Asperger's Syndrome are frequently mis-diagnosed as having attention deficit disorder (ADD) due to initial concerns about concentration among these students. Their need for consistency and their extreme difficulty during conversations are often evidenced in their persistent attempts to redirect conversations to their current areas of intense personal interest. Many people might consider such off-task behavior symptomatic of the daydreaming associated with ADD.

Listening skills, especially in group settings such as a classroom, also evidence deficits for students with Asperger's Syndrome. Teachers often complain that students with Asperger's Syndrome constantly appear to be daydreaming. These children may com-pletely ignore new information, especially new academic information. Without specific training, most students with Asperger's Syndrome don't understand the basic requirement placed on students to pay attention, participate, and learn the information presented in school. The academic agenda is often not one in which these students desire to participate.

It is not uncommon for teachers to describe a particular picture while showing it to the class. Doing so helps to reinforce the auditory mes-sage with a visual prop. This technique is often used throughout the day in countless schools, but this common teaching strategy may present unexpected difficulties for a teacher with Thomas, the tele-phone pole expert, in her classroom. Whereas all students except Thomas may have digested the story or lesson, as demonstrated by their answers, Thomas may have spent the entire time studying the various telephone poles in the picture and completely ignored the lecture. His intent gaze, mistakenly taken by the teacher for rapt attention, was, in fact, directed solely toward his obsessive interest in telephone poles. Instead of focusing on the academic topic, he withdrew into his personal fantasy world.

Many teachers have expressed extreme frustration in discovering that their student with Asperger's Syndrome has spent the entire class time completely ignoring the subject at hand. These teachers fail to recognize that the student is not purposely ignoring them. After all, it was they who presented him with material that aroused his obsessive area of interest.

Reading

Attention to written information presents similar problems for students with Asperger's Syndrome as attending to auditory information. Many of these students have difficulty with reading comprehension. They frequently concentrate on unimportant information and fail to understand the main idea of an article. Recalling facts, selecting important details, predicting logical outcomes, recognizing plot sequence, and determining cause-effect relationships may all be negatively impacted by these students' inability to segment their focus. Their skills for processing and retaining appropriate information are extremely deficient.

Classroom Discussions

This same problem is also present in these children's ability to focus on class discussions. What may appear to be inattentiveness may actually be related to an inability to assign and prioritize importance to the information to which they are trying to attend. It is difficult to attend to oral presentations when all information is viewed as equally important.

This inability to prioritize information causes other difficulties. Since students with Asperger's Syndrome consider all information equally important, they tend to be very disorganized. They do not scan information efficiently when they read. This lack of scanning further compounds their disorganization as they are forced to re-read all information. These students often stuff their papers, notes, and homework inside pockets or jam them into loose-leaf notebooks without regard to due date, completion, or class. Because their information is arranged so haphazardly, these students have difficulty monitoring themselves. They cannot easily review their work without rummaging through numerous papers and often have no idea where they are in relation to a completion date for a project. As a result, their homework is often incomplete.

Time Management and Organization

Time management skills are extremely ineffective for students with Asperger's Syndrome. They have extreme difficulty initiating projects. These students will assume that it is possible to read *War and Peace* overnight and write a fifty-page paper on the book as well. Their ability to procrastinate on assignments is astounding. When they finally do begin to work on a topic or project, they may either rush through it without regard to the quality or timeliness of their work, or persist to work on it well past the completion date. In class, they are often completely distracted from the task at hand. They know their classmates are diligently completing an assignment in class, but because their inability to start the assignment is hampered by their poor time management, these students instead are busy twirling their hair or engaging in some other equally distracting, inappropriate task.

In some instances, students' distractibility may be secondary to organizational and motor coordination problems. Many children with Asperger's Syndrome have significant organizational deficits. They have written down the directions but now have no idea where the directions are. When they finally find the directions, they cannot determine what information may be required to complete the task. This inability to use effective organization skills sets these students apart from their peers, who typically do not have these difficulties.

Motor Difficulties

Fine-motor skill deficits are also common in children with Asperger's Syndrome and are a stated feature in the *ICD-10*'s classification system (see pages 14-15). These motor deficits are immediately evident in the numerous penmanship problems these students exhibit. They often resist the frequent classroom pencil-and-paper tasks. These children know that writing is difficult. They are frustrated that their finished products are typically not to their liking. The speed and dexterity with which these students form letters is well behind their peers' skills. This discrepancy increases these students' frustration because they are almost always the last ones to finish written tasks. In many instances, they never do finish. The constant disappointments associated with these fine-motor deficits often serve to create a defeatist attitude in which these students refuse to participate in writing tasks. Past experience tells them that the outcome will be the same whether they try their hardest or don't try at all.

Some individuals with Asperger's Syndrome have gross-motor deficits as well as fine-motor deficits. When walking down the hall, these students frequently have a stiff gait, making their stride noticeably different from their peers'. Students with Asperger's Syndrome may be excessively clumsy and bump into objects and people. They drop their pencils and books much more often than their peers do. When these students reach into boxes full of items, they inevitably cannot pick out the desired object as easily as their peers can. Recognizing the limitations in their motor skills, students with Asperger's Syndrome are often reluctant to participate in games requiring motor coordination. Kickball, football, basketball, and similar games requiring extensive motor coordination all create significant difficulties for these children. They cannot coordinate their bodies with the same dexterity and precision as their peers. Unfortunately, these games are common physical education activities.

Peers quickly recognize that students with Asperger's Syndrome have coordination difficulties, so the peers are reluctant to pick these students for team sports. As a result, students with Asperger's Syndrome are further humiliated by being the last children to be chosen for sports teams.

Group sports, by their nature, demand social interaction, another weak area for students with Asperger's Syndrome. These students may not participate with the same degree of vigor as their peers or may simply prefer not to participate at all. For individuals with Asperger's Syndrome, kickball is just as much a social threat as it is a motor one.

Robert hates P.E. He hates sports. He hates kickball. Today is P.E. and he is required to participate in kickball. Not wanting to humiliate himself, he tries everything he can think of to avoid participating. He knows he must have adequate eye-hand and eye-foot skills to kick the ball, skills he doesn't have. If he manages to connect with the ball, he must then run to first base before being tagged out, a difficult task due to his poor motor coordination, despite the constant assistance from his physical therapist. If he makes it to first base, he must repeat this feat three more times in an effort to reach home plate to score a point.

Two things go through Robert's mind: "Why bother? I'll never succeed" and "I'm already here at home base. Why do I have to run all over the place just to get back here?" To Robert, both are equally valid points for not participating. To his teammates, Robert is the reason they will lose this game. The resentment builds on both sides.

Students like Robert are well known throughout the school. He is the topic of conversation at many lunch tables and in the hall. Robert tries to be part of the school crowd, but never quite seems to succeed. No matter how hard he tries, Robert never seems to fit in. Students don't want to be with him and teachers give a sigh of relief when they learn he is not in their classes. To teachers, Robert is a difficult student. He is bright and has the intelligence to do the classwork. The reports in his file all indicate his IQ is at or above the norm. Why, then, does he act the way he does?

To teachers, students with Asperger's Syndrome, like Robert, are a puzzle. These students possess average to above-average intelligence, but they never "get it together." They constantly daydream in class and frequently fail to finish their homework. It's as if they simply do not care — and most children with Asperger's Syndrome don't care. That's because the school agenda is not one in which they are interested. Failing to recognize this characteristic of children with Asperger's Syndrome, teachers often complain that these children could do the classwork if they only wanted to. There may be some degree of truth to that statement, since these children do possess the cognitive skills necessary for classroom success. However, they differ from most other children in that their lack of participation is not because of laziness or self-discipline issues.

Comprehension

Another feature of Asperger's Syndrome that many classroom teachers fail to fully appreciate is the presence of comprehension deficits. These students' pedantic speaking style and impressive vocabulary skills mask the fact that they often simply mimic what they have heard. Their impressive vocabulary, good command of syntax, and normal or advanced IQ cause teachers and others to expect too much of these children.

Despite these impressive skills, these students often need and can benefit from support services. Unfortunately, many children with Asperger's Syndrome do not qualify for services because they ordinarily do not exhibit the deficits needed for placement on standardized testing. Formal language testing, especially for adolescents, is often heavily weighted with vocabulary. For children with Asperger's Syndrome, vocabulary is a strength; it is pragmatics that is the major deficit area. In an effort to remain completely objective, many school districts now require standardized instruments to determine eligibility prior to the provision of special services. Unfortunately, these instruments do not adequately tap the true source of the language problems of children with Asperger's Syndrome.

Abstract Thinking

In addition to the pragmatic language problems previously discussed, these children also present with deficits in high-level thinking processes. These deficits cause students with Asperger's Syndrome to have difficulties making decisions and solving problems. Their ability to generate and clarify ideas is limited for their age due to poor abstract thinking. They are typically extremely literal and excel at highly concrete, rote learning tasks. These students do not store information efficiently in the brain. They arrange sequential information haphazardly without any apparent association between memory segments. This scattered storage creates an erratic pattern of performance on academic tasks. In some settings these students are correct, yet in others, they are absolutely wrong. If there is one thing students with Asperger's Syndrome do not want to be, it is "wrong." They absolutely despise making mistakes and can be expected to cause a commotion over errors. This intolerance for errors only serves to further confuse teachers as to the students' true potential.

Inadequate Diagnoses

Children with Asperger's Syndrome generally enter kindergarten not adequately diagnosed. Preschool teachers may have mentioned, or even emphatically stated, their concerns with behavior and social interaction. Those that do enter kindergarten with a label will most likely have diagnoses such as *autism, attention-deficit hyperactivity disorder, emotionally handicapped, learning disabled,* or *language disordered.* While each of these disorders has some aspects similar to Asperger's Syndrome, none completely explains the entire range of strengths and deficits generally seen in this population.

By the time children with Asperger's Syndrome enter kindergarten, their parents are extremely suspicious that something is wrong with them. Many of these children have been reading for quite some time, as hyperlexia is a very common feature of young children with Asperger's Syndrome. Kindergarten readiness testing among children usually indicates excellent performance on rote learned tasks, such as letters, numbers, and basic concepts, but parents have noticed, as have preschool teachers, the immaturity in these children's social skills and peer interactions and continue to express concerns regarding their ability to succeed.

As these students progress through the elementary school years, their academic performance is typically within normal expectations. In most settings they are being educated in the regular education class with typical peers. Teachers begin expressing concern regarding the tendency for verbosity, inadequate social skills, and the inevitable obsessive interests, none of which fit in well within the classroom. Teachers note these students' poor ability to make and keep friends and worry about their desire to watch television or play on the computer while all the other classmates are outside playing. Teachers also comment on these students' poor motor skills, noting the children's difficulty with pencil and crayon tasks. Both the classroom teacher and physical education teacher may have expressed concern regarding inferior gross-motor skills. They also note these students' reluctance to participate in group activities and increasing stubbornness. Some of these students may also exhibit signs of auditory hypersensitivity in large and loud environments.

As these children reach middle school and high school, they may be referred to a diagnostic team to help in educational planning. Typically they receive a label of *learning disabled, attention-deficit hyperactivity disorder*, or *emotionally handicapped*. New labels begin to appear, such as *oppositional-defiant disorder* and *conduct disorder*. As in the elementary years, each of these diagnostic labels has some merit. These students do often have some form of learning problem and their ability to daydream certainly can look like an attention deficit. Their social skills qualify them for an *emotionally handicapped* label. Stubbornness and episodes of rage certainly can indicate *oppositional-defiant disorder* and *conduct disorder*. Unfortunately, educational placement is frequently decided based on these students' behavior, and the outcome may not be in the children's best interests.

Social Interaction

Perhaps the greatest difficulty for students during these years is in the area of social skills. In middle school, the demands for social interaction become even more critical for the student. Unfortunately, this ability to socialize continues to be a puzzle these individuals cannot master. Their inadequate social skills only increase the likelihood that teachers and other students will misunderstand them. Teachers will talk about them in the break room and express their frustration at not being able to figure them out. They have had other students with ADHD and have managed to get through the class without the types of disruptions caused by these students. Why are these students with Asperger's Syndrome so difficult to manage?

These students' peers, who are less tolerant than adults of those who don't conform to expectations, incessantly criticize and tease these youngsters mercilessly. They are most likely left out of social activities by those who either are offended by students with Asperger's Syndrome or by the thought of what others will say if they do try to befriend these inept adolescents. As a result, students with Asperger's Syndrome become frustrated and withdraw from any further attempts at establishing social interactions, instead preferring the routines and rituals that continue to maintain importance. Some of these students may have episodes of behavioral outbursts associated with their inability to establish friendships.

Despite these odds, some individuals with Asperger's Syndrome do manage to establish friendships, often with children who are several years younger than they are. However, some individuals with Asperger's Syndrome establish friendships with other students when their idiosyncratic interests happen to coincide with academic interests. In these situations, students with Asperger's Syndrome may be a sought-after commodity for those seeking to increase their grades. Some individuals with Asperger's Syndrome may discover that others have similar special interests and join corresponding academic clubs, such as a computer club or math club.

During middle school years, students with Asperger's Syndrome may develop an interest in the other sex. However, due to their inability to interact appropriately, they often fail to adequately recognize the emotional response provided by the targets of their infatuation. In their zeal to establish these relationships, students with Asperger's Syndrome may exhibit signs of attentiveness that closely resemble stalking. Their inappropriate conversational skills compound this difficulty. It is not uncommon for these individuals to state what is on their minds without regard to the impact that may have on others. Many high school students with Asperger's Syndrome have found themselves sitting in the office wondering why they were there. The inappropriate comments and actions of some students with Asperger's Syndrome have had dire consequences, some of which have resulted in police investigations.

Despite these potential negative outcomes, most students with Asperger's Syndrome progress through the high school years with the majority of conflicts centering around their inability to adjust socially. They may be labeled as *offensive* or *belligerent*, especially

with respect to accepting other people's opinions. Unstructured social settings, such as those found at dances, pep rallies, physical education classes, and the lunchroom, can create extensive social challenges for these individuals. Their higher-level language problems involving abstract and figurative language together with a poor recognition of idiomatic expressions cause them to continually misunderstand messages. Their responses may be highly exaggerated or completely inappropriate, causing them even further difficulties.

While the outlook for these students appears fraught with challenges not faced by others, most adolescents with Asperger's Syndrome do manage to develop considerable coping strategies that allow them to participate and succeed in what is most likely the most complex environment with which they will be presented. By the time they graduate from high school, they will have had numerous opportunities to reflect upon and refine the manner in which they choose to participate in their environments. The academic demands placed upon them will cease to exist and they will no longer be required to participate in subjects and assignments in which they have limited or no interest. The anxiety associated with these demands will dramatically decrease and, with them, the frequency of emotional outbursts.

➤ Academic Checklist

The Academic Checklist, pages 116-117, is provided to allow you an opportunity to quickly reflect on the various behaviors and skill deficits that may be seen in a student diagnosed with Asperger's Syndrome.

Academic Checklist

Student: _____   Date: _____

School: _____   Evaluator: _____

Check each item that applies to the student in comparison with same-aged peers. The presence of these characteristics or behaviors may suggest the presence of Asperger's Syndrome and/or facilitate selecting appropriate intervention goals. Elaborate with examples or additional comments as warranted.

➤ Academic Issues

- ☐ Does the child lack tact?
- ☐ Does the child often talk off-task?
- ☐ Does the child appear to daydream frequently?
- ☐ Does the child appear to ignore new information?
- ☐ Does the child have difficulty with reading comprehension?
- ☐ Does the child have hyperlexia?
- ☐ Does the child focus on unimportant information?
- ☐ Does the child appear to be disorganized?
- ☐ Does the child have poor self-monitoring skills?
- ☐ Does the child fail to complete classwork in a timely manner?
- ☐ Does the child manage time poorly?

➤ Academic Issues, *continued*

☐ Does the child have difficulty initiating assignments?

☐ Does the child have organizational difficulties?

☐ Does the child have fine-motor problems?

☐ Does the child appear to have a defeatist attitude?

☐ Does the child appear to have gross-motor problems?

☐ Does the child appear to be clumsy?

☐ Does the child appear to have difficulty with eye-hand coordination?

☐ Does the child avoid group sports?

☐ Does the child have a normal or above-normal IQ?

☐ Does the child appear to have poor problem-solving skills?

☐ Does the child appear to have poor abstract reasoning?

☐ Does the child appear to be overly literal?

☐ Does the child's performance seem erratic?

☐ Does the child hate making mistakes?

 # Treatment Strategies

It is difficult for students to learn when they have only a slight interest in academics. Teachers continually describe their students with Asperger's Syndrome as *belligerent* and *unmotivated about school*. They compare these students to the others in the class and remark how difficult they are to teach. These students do not respond in the same manner as their peers. They have an extremely difficult time initiating work and their motivation to participate in class activities is minimal at best. When they finally do begin to engage in academic work, they frequently daydream and are easily distracted. Add to these concerns the fact that many of these children possess poor motor skills. These motor problems directly impede their ability to participate in classroom tasks and also cause extensive emotional turmoil. Despite their strong intelligence, these students frequently do not understand the academic lessons and often require time-consuming individualization. Many teachers have breathed a sigh of relief upon learning that their students with Asperger's Syndrome will be absent that day — more so for an extended illness.

It is no secret that these students require more from the educational system than their peers. Teachers must take these students' unique learning styles and emotional concerns into consideration if these children are to succeed in school. Unfortunately, many of these students are not adequately diagnosed and participate in the school curriculum under misdiagnoses. Teachers often attempt to instruct these students in the style that they have used with similarly labeled students, only to discover that these techniques do not appear to work. What are these teachers supposed to do?

Despite what teachers may think, students like Thomas can be educated quite successfully, given appropriate modifications. What follows is a discussion on various strategies and techniques that have shown promising results in educating children with Asperger's Syndrome.

Engaging in Tasks

Teachers invariably report that their students with Asperger's Syndrome often have a difficult time initiating work. They often gaze everywhere except where they should. When told to start working, these students frequently become obstinate and refuse to participate. At this point, the battle lines have been drawn and the students are not about to capitulate. Teachers and staff now have to decide which avenue to take to reestablish their authority. Further attempts at demanding compliance will inevitably escalate the conflict until an all-out rage episode occurs. Demanding compliance is not recommended; it rarely produces the intended result. Instead, it is more advisable to calmly restate the directives, often adding a tag question; for example, a comment such as "We all are doing our science work and you do want to be like the rest of your classmates, right?" will have a tendency to produce the desired result much more readily than an outright demand, especially if such a directive is spoken in a light, easy, calm manner. It may also be advisable to demonstrate the desired expectation. By seeing a concrete example, the students may realize the task is not as difficult as they thought and begin to comply.

Contingency statements are also an effective way to engage students with Asperger's Syndrome. Simple statements such as "First work, then ___ " are effective, especially when paired with a visual prompt.

For some individuals with Asperger's Syndrome, the basis of the power struggle is in the perception of the amount of work required. In these situations, it may be advisable to segment the workload into smaller units. This segmentation allows the students increased opportunities for breaks between segments as well as the perception that the task is not as long as they originally thought.

In some instances it may be advisable to use a timer, such as the Time Timer™. The students quickly recognize the amount of time required to participate on the task and are more likely to participate. However, some students may find timed tasks, such as those frequently used in math drills, to be too stressful and refuse to allow their use. Timed work sessions, therefore, should be perceived as a set amount of time prior to receiving a break. They should not be used as a period of time in which a set amount of work must be completed.

Consistent Success

Many students with Asperger's Syndrome have developed a defeatist attitude over the years. To help combat this negative attitude, develop opportunities for consistent success. Allowing students to experience situations in which they perceive themselves as successful increases the chances that they will be more receptive to attempting new tasks.

Teachers may also adapt grading expectations for their students with Asperger's Syndrome. Require less from these students initially and gradually increase the quantity of work assigned. Eventually, these students will approximate more normal academic participation and performance.

It would be unreasonable to assume that these strategies will consistently produce the desired results. Difficulties will continue to occur. When they do, it will be necessary to explain and demonstrate several times to help students reduce their frustration. It may also be helpful to anticipate those situations known to create anxiety. In doing so, you can make appropriate modifications to avoid problems. Proactive planning can prevent many obstacles from developing and ultimately create a more enjoyable day for all.

Some students with Asperger's Syndrome may have a difficult time remaining motivated to continue academic tasks. They may begin without problems but quickly tire of the activity or lesson. For these students, create opportunities to enable them to perceive themselves not only as successful, but ready to participate in the assigned activities as well.

Task Completion

Buddy systems allow opportunities for other students to assist the children with Asperger's Syndrome to participate more fully in the academic agenda. Buddy systems are not new. They have been used in most schools for years. Buddy systems can be a major asset for students with Asperger's Syndrome. By providing opportunities for modeling appropriate class behavior and assisting in organizational skills, buddy systems may have a positive impact on the students' behavior, motivation, and social skills.

Buddy systems by themselves will not produce the degree of desired change in these students. Teachers may need to use intermittent verbal and/or physical prompts to ensure the students remain focused and maintain an appropriate attitude toward the tasks presented.

Task lists also help these students to stay organized and remain focused on appropriate steps to complete assignments. Checking off each activity upon completion increases the likelihood of remaining on task. These and other visual strategies assist students in self-monitoring their behavior. The teachers and students can develop subtle prompts based on the needs of the individual students and the class as a whole.

Another technique found to assist in motivating students to continue working is to alternate preferred activities with non-preferred activities. By alternating academic tasks with fun activities, teachers increase the likelihood that students will complete tasks generally considered boring or too difficult. It is much easier to tackle a lengthy project or a series of difficult projects if opportunities are present to lessen the perceived drudgery. For many students with Asperger's Syndrome, these preferred activities may be slight modifications to the general curriculum. Thomas, our telephone pole expert, refused to perform word problems. He found them uninteresting and a useless waste of time. With the same word problems altered to incorporate telephone poles, Thomas now perceives the task as much more meaningful and is more likely to attempt it. The teacher can manipulate his compliance by alternating these modified problems with original ones. By slowly increasing the number of original questions prior to obtaining a modified question, the teacher can fade Thomas's need for the modified questions. This technique is often much more successful in achieving compliance and maintaining motivation than simple demands followed by consequences.

For some students with Asperger's Syndrome, the type of adaptation required may simply be a change in the time of day for a particular subject. Using the visual schedule board to indicate the time of day for each subject may be beneficial, especially if the student is allowed to determine the schedule himself.

Using preferential seating may also help to motivate some students with Asperger's Syndrome. Such preferential seating may be based on location within the room, proximity to a classmate, or some other

factor the students find favorable. Just as their interests may change from day to day with respect to the class schedule, their preferred seats may also change.

Some teachers are concerned that allowing students to determine the location of their seats may increase the potential for distraction. While this concern is valid, it generally is not as much of a concern as motivating students with Asperger's Syndrome to complete the academic tasks they need to accomplish.

Once students with Asperger's Syndrome have been properly motivated, keeping them on task then becomes the teacher's next concern, as these students are often distracted. For many individuals, removing items of distractibility may solve the problem. If a student has an obsessive compulsion to bite on his pencil eraser, it may be easier to remove all pencils or at least only allow pencils without erasers to be used, than to constantly prompt, cue, and cajole him into compliance. For some students, predetermined nonverbal cues may redirect attention focus successfully. Schedule a time to review with each child possible subtle cues you will use to help him recognize when he is off task. Incorporate these prompts within the class setting to allow him to redirect his effort more successfully.

As mentioned previously, presenting academic tasks in a hierarchy of steps motivates students to perform effectively. If students become less inclined to participate and begin to be more distracted, it may be necessary to review the hierarchy and step back, thereby reducing the demand for maintaining attention to tasks the students don't particularly enjoy. Withdrawing the supports previously provided may negatively impact the rate and degree of success obtained. Be aware of what supports were previously provided and consider whether any have been faded too soon. Reintroduce them into the students' day to lessen their distractibility.

Visual representations designed to assist in focusing students' attention to appropriate features may also be incorporated. STOP and GO signs are regularly used on standardized tests as a non-demanding means of increasing compliance. These signs provide an additional means of proactive intervention to help avoid problems. Even though the instructions may be stated orally by the teacher and are printed at the beginning of the test, some students with Asperger's Syndrome may be so engrossed in the task that they fail to heed the directions.

Having a visual prompt to "STOP" in the form of a traffic signal is a relatively easy way to help students focus. Placing these visual symbols in appropriate locations within the text enables students to follow tasks appropriately with greater independence. Other visual prompts, such as arrows, boxes, highlighting, and italicizing, all help students to focus on tasks and resist distractions. Teachers may also increase attention to oral directions by signaling the class with an appropriate cue prior to providing instructions. Simple prompts such as "Watch my lips" or "Listen up" have all produced gains in auditory comprehension. A unique by-product of this technique is that all the students can benefit from its use.

Reading Comprehension

Many teachers encountering students with Asperger's Syndrome have erroneously overestimated these students' reading comprehension skills. Their extremely varied, large vocabulary masks their difficulty in understanding what they read. To assist these students in developing their reading comprehension, it may be advisable to pair written information with pictures whenever possible. This strategy will not only enable students to grasp written material better, it will also help to maintain their attention.

Highlighting key words in text also is helpful. Many textbooks commonly employ this technique. Key vocabulary words are frequently written in bold or italicized type to draw greater attention to them. Due to their organizational deficits, students with Asperger's Syndrome frequently have difficulty ascribing different layers of importance to written words. Highlighting target words allows these students to develop greater skills in deciphering which words are important and which are not. Abstract concepts, such as metaphors and idioms, cause extensive difficulty for these students. Specific instruction in learning how to recognize metaphors and idioms and their implied meanings will also benefit these students.

Study guides have also been found to aid students with Asperger's Syndrome. These guides, developed by the classroom teacher or some other individual familiar with the information, present the academic material in an abbreviated format to allow students to

relate to the information in another format besides just text paragraphs. Written outlines, study questions, and bulleted highlights of information to learn are examples of study guides that may help students understand what they read.

A frustrating characteristic of students with Asperger's Syndrome is the tendency to project their personal experiences or emotions into what they read. To reduce errors associated with this faulty reasoning, it may be advisable to ask these students where in the written material a fact was illustrated. Repeatedly questioning students to show proof of where they obtained information not only reduces errors but also teaches these students a valuable technique for understanding what they read.

Specific instruction should also be provided to assist the student in learning how to draw plausible conclusions to stories. Students with Asperger's Syndrome typically project their personal beliefs into stories they read, ignoring the actual story. This practice creates significant difficulty when these students are required to predict or support the logical conclusion of these stories. With specific instruction, these students can learn to draw plausible conclusions for stories. Teach them to locate the facts and the sequencing of plot events within the stories. Ask these students to specify the information in the stories that supports any conclusions or inferences they make.

Summarizing stories is also difficult for students with Asperger's Syndrome. This difficulty is partly due to their projection of personal ideas or values into what they read. When these students are asked to summarize stories, they may focus on unimportant details or incorporate a personal experience or belief. A visual-tactile support may help these students focus their story summations. Teach the students to use their fingers as guides to sequence story information. For example, the thumb represents *What happened first* and the pinky represents *What happened last*. The middle finger is for *What happened in the middle*. The index and ring finger represent *What happened between the beginning and the middle* and *What happened between the middle and the ending*, respectively. By consistently using this technique to instruct story sequencing, teachers may witness students spontaneously employing its use thereby achieving greater accuracy in story sequencing and summarizing skills.

Some students with Asperger's Syndrome have an extremely difficult time recognizing when they are off task and distracted. Despite being told that they are not focusing their attention on the appropriate task, they may not agree or be able to process the reasoning through auditory input alone. For these individuals, it may be beneficial to use videotaping as an opportunity to demonstrate appropriate and inappropriate attending styles. Similar to social autopsies, videotaping provides both visual and auditory feedback to enable students to determine if they were truly on task or not.

Motor Deficits

Many students with Asperger's Syndrome show symptoms of distractibility or refusal to participate that, when analyzed, are actually behaviors secondary to gross-motor deficits. Teachers should be alert to these deficits and consider whether such factors explain poor task performance or participation.

It is unrealistic to assume that students with Asperger's Syndrome can handle competitive sports. The presence of motor planning problems and social deficits creates a wide range of difficulties not seen in the general population. For these students, it may be more advantageous to offer adaptive physical educational activities. Eliminating the interpersonal competitiveness associated with traditional sports may facilitate greater interest, participation, and performance. In addition to adaptive sports, referral for occupational or physical therapy may be warranted to assist these students in developing better motor planning skills.

Students with fine-motor problems may find cursive handwriting an easier method of writing than printing. The ease with which the letters flow from one another appears to reduce the frustration associated with printing. The increased time required for these students to complete pencil-and-paper tasks often increases the likelihood of frustration associated with fatigue. Their motor deficits do not allow them to keep up with their classmates and they are inevitably the last to finish. Unless opportunities are provided to lessen this frustration, behavioral situations will ultimately result.

Frequent breaks from writing have been found to significantly reduce this degree of frustration. As a result, extending the time in which assignments are to be completed is highly recommended. Unfortunately for the student, these issues in penmanship have a tendency to be reflected in their grades. Teachers do not appreciate struggling through illegible assignments and often show their displeasure through grades. The wise instructor knows that these students' deficient legibility is not a function of indifference, but rather is secondary to yet another trait of Asperger's Syndrome. It would be no more appropriate to downgrade a child with a visual impairment for not adequately reading from the board than it would be to downgrade a student with Asperger's Syndrome for producing what is affectionately known as "sloppy copy."

Situations in which penmanship problems create extensive difficulties may be best resolved by eliminating the need to write responses by hand. Here are some options to consider:

➤ Word processors are an excellent choice for response delivery. They are available in many price ranges, depending upon the size and features offered.

➤ Allow students to substitute oral responses for written responses, thereby bypassing the anxiety-producing frustration of writing responses.

➤ When direct presentation is not feasible, let students tape record responses for review at a later date instead.

No matter which technique is used to minimize the need to write by hand, it is most important for these students to be able to participate in classroom lessons and activities. Teachers should allow these students to employ whatever adaptive techniques benefit them to achieve this goal.

Adapting the Curriculum

Many students with Asperger's Syndrome may require adaptation of the general curriculum. No single academic curriculum is appropriate for every individual, and modifying the curriculum to capitalize on students' interests is relatively easy.

Some curricula are more heavily laden with reading comprehension and critical thinking than others. Curricula that employ these learning styles will certainly disadvantage the student with Asperger's Syndrome because these students are normally weak in these areas. It may be necessary to simplify the abstract lessons found within this style of curriculum. If this simplification fails to produce the desired result, it may be wise to substitute the curriculum with one that relies less on critical thinking and more on factual knowledge.

Modifying the Environment

Modifying the academic environment is always advisable when working with students with Asperger's Syndrome. Few classroom teachers are capable of providing the degree of direct intervention required by these students because of other teaching demands across the classroom. Teachers may find it beneficial to utilize support staff as much as possible to offer these students more individualized learning. While support staff provide greater opportunities for individualized learning to take place, they can also have a positive impact on the students' self-confidence. Individualizing the curriculum and instructional methods greatly increase the ability of students with Asperger's Syndrome to participate and learn successfully within the classroom environment.

Many students with Asperger's Syndrome require specific modifications of homework or other assignments to enable them to fully complete assignments without struggling with undue anxiety. Teachers are often completely unaware of the amount of time parents and children need to complete written essays. They know that students like Thomas will need more time than the rest of the class to complete the assignment. However, few teachers have actually watched a child labor at home over a written assignment from start to finish. Doing so would provide a wonderful opportunity for teachers to be more empathic with students' needs and abilities.

One suggestion for modifying written assignments is to allow students to create an outline instead of an essay in paragraphs. This modification minimizes deficits in fine-motor skills that make lengthy writing assignments a nightmare for some students.

Essay tests present similar difficulties. The increased processing time required to produce the written material is frequently longer than that allowed. Providing extra time to complete the assignment may not be in students' best interests. In this situation, it may be more advisable to use multiple-choice tests rather than essay tests.

Many teachers realize that students such as Thomas require additional time in just about everything they do. For these students, it may be beneficial to shorten assignments to allow greater opportunities for success. Adapting academic tasks by adjusting the type of questions and the number of items students are expected to master may improve these students' performance.

Likewise, other students may need adaptations of the amount of time they participate in a lesson. The social difficulties and obsessive interests associated with Asperger's Syndrome may overload these students' adequate cognitive skills. In order to monitor and control their social and obsessive issues, these children often need to exert the same amount of cognitive effort typical students use for academic purposes. Assuming that these students are capable of fully participating in academic lessons is expecting too much of them; they simply don't have the extra energy to stay on task and learn as readily as other students.

It may be advisable to slowly increase the amount of time students with Asperger's Syndrome are expected to participate in class discussions as the degree of cognitive effort required to remain focused on these discussions is extremely intense. For those not challenged with Asperger's Syndrome, this task may not seem too difficult, but for students with Asperger's Syndrome, the effort required for classroom discussions is extraordinary. Like their peers, they have difficulty with the topic and frequently do not find it of any interest. Additionally, students with Asperger's Syndrome have difficulty understanding multiple-meaning words, implied meaning, abstraction, and academic terminology. Many also have difficulties with fine-motor skills, making note-taking laborious and frustrating. Looming over everything these students do is the ever-constant fear of social ineptness and the anxiety it produces. Expecting students with Asperger's Syndrome to consistently participate in whole-class discussions is unrealistic. The degree of self-control required to maintain composure for the entire class time may be too much of a burden. Increase the amount of time they are expected to participate gradually to ensure success and build self-confidence.

Teachers also must realize the need to adapt their presentation style. Those who incorporate audio-visual materials will have a much greater chance of keeping the attention of their students, including those with Asperger's Syndrome. Overhead projectors have shown to hold students' interest far more than chalkboard use alone. Even though they both present the same information on a wall, students with Asperger's Syndrome appear to attend to the overhead projector more than the chalkboard.

Another effective teaching modification, though cumbersome, is to give students prewritten notes of teaching presentations. Although some teachers may initially be unwilling to adopt this presentation method, they may eventually appreciate the resulting improved comprehension for their students.

In addition to the above adaptations, teachers must recognize the need to paraphrase all information they present orally. This type of repetition of information presented enhances all students' comprehension and is essential for students with Asperger's Syndrome.

Thinking Skills

The cognitive processing skills present in individuals with Asperger's Syndrome are uniquely different from their peers' skills. As reported previously, individuals with Asperger's Syndrome have excellent syntax and semantics but evidence deficiencies in both critical thinking and the recognition and use of abstract language. If gains are to be achieved in overall cognitive processing, it becomes necessary to provide assistance in a wide variety of areas within the domain of cognitive processing, not just isolated areas. Critical thinking, the ability to apply reasoning and inference to newly acquired information, is an extremely difficult area for these individuals. Techniques designed to assist in processing critical thinking skills, as well as the recognition and use of abstract language, will promote more effective cognitive processing.

Many individuals with Asperger's Syndrome possess exceptional memory for facts. It is not uncommon for students with Asperger's Syndrome to know the names of dinosaurs or every Nintendo™ game ever marketed. Their uncanny ability to remember information of

this type is truly remarkable, but their ability to apply this information during social conversations may be noticeably poor. Having an encyclopedic knowledge of data does not make one academically advanced. These students often need direct instruction in how to apply their exceptional memory skills more meaningfully.

Unfortunately, some individuals with Asperger's Syndrome have difficulty in memorizing material for use in academic situations. This weakness is especially true in subjects where the students have minimal interest. Specific techniques for improving memory for academic information may be required for these individuals to keep up with academic requirements. Countless people use mnemonic devices every day. For example, the classic *Thirty days hath September, April, June, and November* is widely known and successfully employed to this day. The success of this particular device is in the use of rhyme and cadence, both of which assist in the retention process.

However, mnemonic devices are not limited to rhyme. Students can learn to make acronyms by employing the first letter of each target word to form a new word. A common acronym is *HOMES* in which each letter represents the names of the five Great Lakes (Huron, Ontario, Michigan, Erie, and Superior). This technique can be elaborated further to produce acronymic sentences. They differ from simple acronyms on the basis that instead of producing a specific word (e.g., *HOMES*), they produce a sentence in which the first letter of the target word is represented by the first letter of each word in the sentence. The trick to using acronymic sentences is to use visualization. The more outlandish these sentences are, the greater the opportunity to retrieve the desired information. For example, the sentence *Miss Veronica Evans made JELL-O stick under Nora's plate* might be used to remember the nine planets: Mercury, Venus, Earth, Mars, Jupiter, Saturn, Uranus, Neptune, and Pluto. The simplicity of acronyms affords a unique opportunity to capitalize on students' rote memory strength by incorporating areas of interest within the acronym. Once the students see the results of these techniques, they may be motivated to incorporate mnemonic devices into their study skills.

Students with Asperger's Syndrome benefit from appropriate classroom organizational strategies. Simple organization in the layout of the classroom's structure may afford many students an opportunity to

develop a greater sense of recognition of space. Maintaining consistency in the location of items required throughout the day helps students with Asperger's Syndrome to reduce the degree of anxiety associated with worrying about the necessary items to complete a task and where to find them.

This kind of consistent physical organization also allows teachers to gradually introduce transitions in such a manner that the associated elevations in stress are managed appropriately. Children with Asperger's Syndrome do not take well to transitions. Excessive care must be undertaken to ensure that transitions are presented in such a manner that the students realize anticipated start-stop times and know beforehand what lies ahead. Visual supports can be a major help in accomplishing smooth transitions with minimal stress. It is extremely beneficial to incorporate a wide variety of visual supports into all daily activities.

Comprehension skills among students with Asperger's Syndrome are typically deficient when compared to the general population. Despite a strong IQ, excellent command of vocabulary, and an uncanny ability to talk forever about particular topics, these students frequently have deficits in both auditory comprehension and reading comprehension. Too often teachers assume these students have fully understood directions and/or class discussions, only to find them completely off task or emotionally agitated. It is extremely important for all who work with these children to ensure that comprehension is truly occurring. Repetition of directions and simplified oral language all improve auditory comprehension for these students. Reading comprehension may be scrutinized by employing numerous spot checks to ensure appropriate learning is taking place. To assist in reading comprehension, instruct students about specific strategies designed to increase reading comprehension. Highlighting while reading is an effective strategy. Unfamiliar words, directions, target words, and other important concepts may all be highlighted to draw attention to them.

Structured lessons may be given to help students recognize vocabulary that often causes confusion on tests. For example, true-false questions typically are false if they contain the terms *always*, *never*, *all*, or similar terminology. Likewise, strategies can also be taught to determine fact from opinion. Facts typically can be answered with a *yes-no* question; opinions frequently cannot. Strategies such as these

all aid in developing greater reading comprehension and, ultimately, better performance on tests.

Math word problems are notoriously difficult for many students. For students with Asperger's Syndrome, these problems pose additional difficulties that require consistent instruction in order to master. Besides teaching the language of math, it may be wise to offer simple word problems based on easy computation to increase the comprehension required to understand the language of math. Pair a simple word problem with a computational task to help students more easily associate the relationship between the two. For example, the number sentence *2 + 2 = ___* may be paired with *John has 2 balls and Mike has 2 balls. How many balls do they have in all?* This technique of simultaneous instruction increases students' ability to solve word problems accurately.

Many students with Asperger's Syndrome have an extremely difficult time with critical thinking. These individuals remain overly focused on concrete facts because there is little room for interpretation. Abstract thought processes must be addressed to improve these students' critical-thinking skills. These students need direct instruction to learn how to think the way the general population does. Conduct brainstorming sessions in which the students are instructed to generate ideas for a given topic, producing possibilities to solve situations. Recognizing and producing metaphoric expressions also enhances thinking skills. Vague responses can be addressed by incorporating techniques to clarify ideas. Comparing and contrasting, classifying, and sequencing are beneficial skills to employ when clarification is required. Thinking skills may be further enhanced by specific instruction in how to develop reasons, conclusions, and assumptions based on information provided.

Another approach to develop higher-level thinking skills is specific instruction in learning how to assess specific information to determine potential causal factors. Students with Asperger's Syndrome often attempt to create an all-or-none scenario. Thinking about possible causes helps these students recognize that multiple options, scenarios, and hypotheses can exist and may be equally valid.

The abilities to predict, generalize, and solve analogies may require direct instruction for students with Asperger's Syndrome. For example, present pictures of social situations and ask students to

predict what may happen next or who probably caused a problem to develop. These tasks can then be generalized by having students describe personal situations where similar circumstances took place.

Analogies often create difficulty because they require students to comprehend the relationship between two words and then choose another word based on the exact relationship. For example, in the analogy *bird : feather :: fish : __?__* , responses such as "tail, fins, gills," etc., may seem appropriate on the surface, as they are all parts of the whole. However, the term *feather* is more than just a part; it is the animal's body covering. Therefore, the correct answer should be *scales*. Some students may produce this answer readily, but other students may require numerous, similar examples before they truly comprehend the relationship between the first two words.

For many students with Asperger's Syndrome, the ability to make appropriate decisions is hampered by an inability to fully recognize the cause-effect relationship between their actions (or lack thereof) and the responses of others. Blurting out, "You're fat!" is a definite social blunder, no matter how obese the individual is. Students with Asperger's Syndrome might typically make the above statement without realizing the impending problem it will most definitely create. Formal instruction in recognizing good and bad social/tact decisions is a necessity for these students because they do not often spontaneously recognize or learn from their errors. Developing students' higher-level thinking skills affords these students more effective tools for making appropriate decisions and solving everyday problems.

Thinking skills may also be enhanced through the use of Bloom's Taxonomy of Educational Objectives (Hawkes et al., 1992). This approach to developing thinking skills is based on the supposition that when people learn new information, they use three different styles, or domains, known as the *affective, psychomotor*, and *cognitive*. The affective domain deals with emotions and feelings. The psychomotor domain is concerned with physical motor skills and dexterity. The cognitive domain emphasizes outcomes based on intellect. Each of these domains is divided further into six categories. Instructing students with Asperger's Syndrome in techniques that incorporate the cognitive domain develops better critical-thinking skills for these individuals.

Teaching students with Asperger's Syndrome to solve logic problems improves not only their critical thinking but also their reading comprehension. In logic problems, students must critically read information to determine missing information and, through deductive reasoning, determine new information. An example of a logic problem is *Mary, Mrs. Smith, and the girl with the orange dress ate at the cafeteria on Tuesday*. From this information, it can be deduced that three individuals ate at the cafeteria on Tuesday. It may be further deduced that Mary's last name is not *Smith* and neither she nor Mrs. Smith wore an orange dress when they went out to eat. Teach students to use a grid to record the information obtained from the problem. Here is an example:

	Orange Dress	Last Name Smith	Ate in Cafeteria
Mary			X
Mrs. Smith		X	X
girl	X		X

Creating a grid enables students to focus on significant information and to learn new information via a process of elimination. The same grid technique is also effective in helping students solve their own everyday problems.

Unwritten Rules at School

Problem solving is extremely difficult when the rules for determining the correct response are "unwritten." Most students learn these unwritten rules quickly when they first go to school. They learn that using a specific bathroom is an invitation to trouble. They learn which teacher they can joke with and which one is always dead serious. They learn what each teacher's expectations are and

Chapter 7: Academic Issues
The Source for Asperger's Syndrome   134   Copyright © 2002 LinguiSystems, Inc.

that few teachers have similar expectations. They learn who's "in" and who's not, which students to avoid, and which to interact with. These skills are not provided in any student handbook or orientation meeting. Teachers and staff do not instruct students about where the athletes or delinquents hang out. Yet, within a few days of school starting, almost every student has learned this information. While these unwritten rules may not carry the same official weight as information within the student handbook, the knowledge of these unwritten rules is extremely important for all students to acquire.

Unfortunately, students with Asperger's Syndrome often fail to recognize these rules and quickly suffer the consequences for their ignorance. To avoid consistent problems in this area, it is extremely important to help students with Asperger's Syndrome to quickly recognize areas and individuals within the school that may be labeled as *safe* and *dangerous*. Maps, comic-strip conversations, and social stories may all be used to assist these students learn the unwritten rules of the school environment.

➤ Teaching Techniques

The following Teaching Techniques, pages 136-139, summarize the techniques reviewed in this chapter. They are provided for your convenience in considering appropriate teaching modifications for students with Asperger's Syndrome.

➢ Teaching Techniques

Helping Students with Assignments

➢ Have a positive attitude.

➢ Remain calm.

➢ Use the universal *we*, as in "We are all doing our math now."

➢ Demonstrate expectations.

➢ Use contingency statements, such as "*First* do your math, *then* use the computer."

➢ Segment work assignments.

➢ Use timed work sessions.

➢ Use consistent successes to help the student make appropriate decisions.

➢ Lower or simplify grading expectations initially and gradually increase expectations.

➢ When difficulties occur, explain and demonstrate to reduce frustration.

➢ Anticipate and avoid anxiety-producing situations.

Increasing Motivation

➢ Use a buddy system.

➢ Employ intermittent verbal or physical prompts.

➢ Use a task list detailing things to do to complete the task.

➢ Use visual prompts when presenting oral information.

➢ Alternate preferred with non-preferred activities.

➢ Schedule tests during the best time of day for the student.

➤ Adapt the curriculum to incorporate the student's interests.

➤ Use preferential seating.

Staying on Task

➤ Use agreed-upon nonverbal cues for redirection.

➤ Minimize the student's injection of personal ideas into academic tasks.

➤ Use a hierarchy of tasks to redirect focus.

➤ Limit distractions.

➤ Videotape the student and "autopsy" to help the student monitor on/off task behavior.

➤ Use "STOP/GO" signs to guide the student through information or pages.

➤ Use arrows, boxes, highlighting, italicizing, bold type, etc., to highlight key information or terms.

➤ Pair words with pictures to enhance comprehension.

➤ Teach the student ways to monitor the remaining time allotted for tasks.

➤ Signal students to pay attention before you give directions.

➤ Allow extended time to complete assignments.

➤ Provide study guides (annotated notes provided by the teacher and given to the student to assist him in studying).

Compensating for Gross-Motor Deficits

➤ Competitive sports will require adaptation.

➤ Consider adaptive PE.

➤ Refer for physical therapy, if appropriate.

Compensating for Fine-Motor Deficits

➢ Encourage using cursive rather than printing.

➢ Offer breaks during writing tasks to reduce fatigue and frustration.

➢ Grade written assignments on content, not proficiency of print.

➢ Allow extended time to complete assignments.

➢ Accept oral responses instead of written; consider allowing tape-recorded responses.

➢ Equip the student with a word processor.

➢ Refer for occupational therapy, if appropriate.

Adapting the Curriculum

➢ Make substitutions in the standard curriculum as necessary.

➢ Modify the curriculum to capitalize on the student's interests.

➢ Simplify abstract lessons.

Academic Modifications

➢ Utilize support staff for more individualized instruction.

➢ Require outlines rather than essays.

➢ Adapt math tasks to real-life, relevant situations.

➢ Give multiple-choice tests rather than essay tests.

➢ Shorten assignments.

➢ Reduce the number of things the student is expected to master.

➢ Adapt the time allotted for tasks.

➢ Adapt the requirement for the student's degree of participation.

➢ Adapt teaching presentation style as necessary.

> Provide direct assistance.

> Paraphrase information presented orally.

Improving Thinking Skills

> Capitalize on exceptional memory skills.

> Teach the use of mnemonic devices.

> Introduce transitions gradually.

> Keep the classroom layout and structure well organized and consistent.

> Use consistency in the location of items in the classroom.

> Incorporate visuals into daily activities.

> Monitor the student's reading comprehension.

> Use simple language to present information orally.

> Repeat and paraphrase directions.

> Incorporate Bloom's Taxonomy in teaching.

> Teach logic problems; use grids.

> Teach "unwritten rules" at school.

> Teach the student to use five fingers (1-5-3-2-4) to summarize a story.

> Teach the student how to draw plausible conclusions to stories.

> Teach critical thinking, especially abstract thought.

> Teach idioms and figurative language.

> Produce simple word problems for computation to increase comprehension of word problems.

Chapter 8:
Prognosis

Outcome predictions with respect to individuals with Asperger's Syndrome remain highly varied. When compared to classical autism, the outlook is much brighter. However, even in the best of situations, deficits will always be present. Social interaction will most likely create the greatest area of difference for these individuals and they will frequently be perceived as somewhat eccentric. As they reach adulthood, many will have established unique coping mechanisms to assist them in their daily activities. The dilemmas associated with adolescence will be behind them and life will seem more consistent and predictable.

"...compared to classical autism, the outlook is much brighter."

Many individuals will obtain employment in settings matching their unique strengths and obsessive interests. For these individuals, the outcomes are extremely positive. However, if individuals are placed in settings that do not tolerate their idiosyncratic peculiarities, problems are bound to occur. For these individuals, the outlook will most likely be poor, involving frequent social infractions and consistent misunderstandings. These people will not conform to normal expectations, so the perceived gap between *different* and *normal* will widen. The individuals with Asperger's Syndrome will be well aware of their *different* status and feel very isolated.

Social interaction for most people with Asperger's Syndrome is a source of lifelong frustration and confusion. Sometimes this prolonged confusion and the social chaos associated with it give rise to secondary psychiatric diagnoses. Psychiatric comorbidity is not uncommon within the Asperger's Syndrome population. Some of the adults may present with paranoia and depression that, if unchecked, may result in suicidal inclination. Obsessive tendencies may increase and become clinically significant, thereby constituting a secondary diagnosis of *obsessive-compulsive disorder*. These obsessions may create further difficulties for the individuals. Criminal concerns among this population frequently center around severe behaviors associated with untreated obsessive-compulsive disorder.

Despite these odds, individuals with Asperger's Syndrome can, and often do, function well within society. Their characteristic differences create a greater range of personalities and traits unique to the human species. It would bode well for us all if we embraced these differences in a warm, accepting manner, rather than cause further emotional turmoil to both ourselves and those challenged with the traits known as *Asperger's Syndrome*.

■　■　■

References

American Psychiatric Association, Ed. (1994). *1994 Diagnostic and Statistical Manual of Mental Disorders.* Washington, D.C.

Asarnow, R., Tanguay, P., Bott, E., and Freeman, B. (1987). "Patterns of intellectual functioning in non-retarded autistic and schizophrenic children." *Journal of Child Psychology and Psychiatry.* **28**: 273-280.

Asperger, H. (1944). "Die 'autistischen psychopathen' im kindersalter." *Archiv fur Psychiatric und Nervenkrankheiten.* **117**: 76-136.

Atwood, T. (1998). *Asperger's Syndrome: A Guide for Parents and Professionals.* London: Jessica Kingsley Publishers.

Baron-Cohen, S., Allen, J., and Gillberg, C. (1992). "Can autism be detected at 18 months? The needle, the haystack, and the CHAT." *British Journal of Psychiatry*, **161**: 839-843.

Baron-Cohen, S., Leslie, A. M., and Frith, U. (1985). "Does the autistic child have a Theory of Mind?" *Cognition.* **21**: 81-90.

Barrett, M., Huisingh, R., Zachman, L., Blagden, C., and Orman, J. (1992). *The Listening Test.* East Moline, IL: LinguiSystems.

Bejerot, S., Nylander, L., and Lindstrom, E. (2001). "Autistic traits in obsessive-compulsive disorder." *Nordic Journal of Psychiatry.* **55**(3): 169-76.

Bieber, J. P. (1994). "Learning disabilities and social skills with Richard LaVoie: Last one picked . . . first one picked on." Washington, D.C.: Public Broadcasting Service.

Bonus, B., Assion, H. J., et al. (1997). "[Coincidence of epilepsy and Asperger syndrome. Case report and review]." *Nervenarzt.* **68**(9): 759-64.

Church, C., Alisanski, S., and Amanullah, S. (2000). "The social, behavioral, and academic experiences of children with Asperger syndrome." *Focus on Autism and Other Developmental Disabilities.* **15**(1): 12-20.

Cumine, V., Leach, J., and Stevenson, G. (1998). *Asperger Syndrome. A Practical Guide for Teachers.* London: David Fulton Publishers.

Dauner, I. and Martin, M. (1978). "[Autism Asperger of early schizophrenia (author's transl)]." *Padiatrie and Padologie.* **13**(1): 31-8.

Dunn, W., Myles, B., Orr, S. (2002). "Sensory processing issues associated with Asperger syndrome: a preliminary investigation." *American Journal of Occupational Therapy.* **56**(1): 97-102.

Dyck, M., Ferguson, K., Shochet, I. (2001). "Do autism spectrum disorders differ from each other and from non-spectrum disorders on emotion recognition tests?" *European Child and Adolescent Psychiatry.* **10**(2): 106-116.

Ehlers, S. and Gillberg, C. (1993). "The epidemiology of Asperger syndrome: a total population study." *Journal of Child Psychology and Psychiatry.* **34**(8): 1327-50.

Ehlers, S., Gillberg, C., et al. (1999). "A screening questionnaire for Asperger syndrome and other high-functioning autism spectrum disorders in school age children." *Journal of Autism and Developmental Disorders.* **29**(2): 129-41.

Ehlers, S., Nyden, A., et al. (1997). "Asperger syndrome, autism and attention disorders: a comparative study of the cognitive profiles of 120 children." *Journal of Child Psychology and Psychiatry.* **38**(2): 207-17.

Ehlers, S., Nyden, A., Gillberg, C., Sandberg, A., Dahlgren, S., Hjelmquist, E., and Oden, A. (1997). "Asperger syndrome, autism and attention disorders: a comparative study of the cognitive profiles of 120 children." *Journal of Child Psychology and Psychiatry.* **38**(2): 207-217.

Eisenmajer, R., Prior, M., et al. (1996). "Comparison of clinical symptoms in autism and Asperger's disorder." *Journal of the American Academy of Child Adolescent Psychiatry.* **35**(11): 1523-31.

Eisenmajer, R., Prior, M., et al. (1998). "Delayed language onset as a predictor of clinical symptoms in pervasive developmental disorders." *Journal of Autism and Developmental Disorders.* **28**(6): 527-33.

Eller, N. S. (1992). *125 Ways to Be a Better Listener.* East Moline, IL: LinguiSystems.

Fombonne, E. (1996). "Is the prevalence of autism increasing?" *Journal of Autism and Developmental Disorders.* **26**(6): 673-6.

Freeman, B., Ritvo, E., Yokota, A., and Ritvo, A. (1986). "A scale for rating symptoms of patients with the syndrome of autism in real life settings." *Journal of the American Academy of Child Psychiatry.* **25**: 130-136.

Gardner, M. (1990). *Expressive One-Word Picture Vocabulary Test.* Novato, CA: Academic Therapy Publications.

Ghaziuddin, M. and Gerstein, L. (1996). "Pedantic speaking style differentiates Asperger syndrome from high-functioning autism." *Journal of Autism and Developmental Disorders.* **26**(6): 585-95.

Gillberg, C. (1991). "Outcome in autism and autistic-like conditions." *Journal of the American Academy of Child Adolescent Psychiatry.* **30**(3): 375-82.

Gillberg, C. and Billstedt, E. (2000). "Autism and Asperger syndrome: coexistence with other clinical disorders." *Acta Psychiatrica Scandinavica.* **102**(5): 321-30.

Gillberg, C., Rastam, M., and Wentz, E. (2001). "The Asperger Syndrome (and high-functioning autism) Diagnostic Interview (ASDI): a preliminary study of a new structured clinical interview." *Autism: The International Journal of Research and Practice.* **5**(1): 57-66.

Gillberg, I. C. and Gillberg, C. (1989). "Asperger syndrome — some epidemiological considerations: a research note." *Journal of the American Academy of Child Adolescent Psychiatry.* **30**(4): 631-8.

Gray, C. (1994). *Comic strip conversations: Colorful, illustrated interactions with students with autism and related disorders.* Jenison, MI: Jenison Public Schools.

Gray, C. (1995). *Social stories unlimited: Social stories and comic strip conversations*. Jenison, MI: Jenison Public Schools.

Green, J., Gilchrist, A., Burton, D., and Cox, A. (2000). "Social and psychiatric functioning in adolescents with Asperger syndrome compared with conduct disorder." *Journal of Autism and Developmental Disorders*. **30**(4): 279-93.

Grice, H. P. (1975). "Logic and conversation." In *Syntax and Semantics*, edited by P. Cole and J. L. Morgan. New York, NY: Academic Press.

Hawkes, R. R., Montgomery, J. L., and McKay, J. W. (1992). *Mastermind for the Primary Grades: Exercises in Critical Thinking*. Glenview, IL: GoodYearBooks.

Kadesjo, B. and Gillberg, C. (2000). "Tourette's disorder: epidemiology and comorbidity in primary school children." *Journal of the American Academy of Child Adolescent Psychiatry*. **39**(5): 548-55.

Kadesjo, B., Gillberg, C., and Hagberg, B. (1999). "Brief report: autism and Asperger syndrome in seven-year-old children: a total population study." *Journal of Autism and Developmental Disorders*. **29**(4).

Kanner, L. (1943). "Autistic disturbances of affective contact." *Nervous Child*. **2**: 217-250.

Klin, A., Sparrow, S., Marans, W., Carter, A., and Volkmar, F. (2000). "Assessment issues in children and adolescents with Asperger syndrome." In *Asperger Syndrome*, edited by A. Klin, F. Volkmar, and S. Sparrow. New York, NY: The Guilford Press.

Lord, C., Rutter, M., Goode, S., Heemsbergen, J., Jordan, H., Mawhood, L., and Schopler, E. (1989). "Autism Diagnostic Observation Schedule: a standardized observation of communicative and social behavior." *Journal of Autism and Developmental Disorders*. **19**: 185-197.

Lord, C., Rutter, M., Le Couteur, A. (1994). "Autism Diagnostic Interview - Revised: a revised version of a diagnostic interview for caregivers of individuals with possible pervasive developmental disorders." *Journal of Autism and Developmental Disorders*. **24**(5): 659-685.

Matese, M., Matson, J., and Sevin, J. (1994). "Comparison of psychotic and autistic children using behavioral observation." *Journal of Autism and Developmental Disorders*. **24**(1): 83-94.

Mayes, S. D. and Calhoun, S. L. (2001). "Non-significance of early speech delay in children with autism and normal intelligence and implications for DSM-IV Asperger's disorder." *Autism: The International Journal of Research and Practice*. **5**(1): 81-94.

McKenna, K., Gordon, C. T., et al. (1994). "Looking for childhood-onset schizophrenia: the first 71 cases screened." *Journal of the American Academy of Child Adolescent Psychiatry*. **33**(5): 636-44.

Miller, J. (1981). *Assessing Language Production in Children*. Baltimore, MD: University Park Press.

O'Neil, J. (1999). "A syndrome with a mix of skills." *New York Times*. New York City, NY: The New York Times Company.

Prutting, C. A. (1983). "Applied Pragmatics." In *Pragmatic Assessment and Intervention Issues in Language*, edited by T. M. Gallagher and C. A. Prutting. San Diego, CA: College-Hill.

Raja, M. and Azzoni, A. (2001). "Asperger's disorder in the emergency psychiatric setting." *General Hospital Psychiatry*. **23**(5): 285-293.

Richard, G. and Hanner, M. (1995). *Language Processing Test–Revised*. East Moline, IL: LinguiSystems.

Ryan, M. (1992). "Treatment-resistant chronic mental illness: is it Asperger's syndrome?" *Hospital Community Psychiatry*. **43**(8): 807-11.

Schopler, E., Mesibov, G. B., and Hearsey, K. (1995). "Structured teaching in the TEACCH system." In *Learning and Cognition in Autism*, edited by E. Schopler and G. Mesibov. New York, NY: Plenum Press.

Schopler, E., Reichler, R., Bashford, A., Lansing, M., and Marcus, L. (1990). *Psychoeducational Profile–Revised (PEP-R)*. Austin, TX: Pro-Ed.